GCSE Music
OCR Areas of Study

- Works seamlessly with the CGP Music Core Content book

- Clear and concise

- 99.8% bagpipe free

Contents

Section Four — Area of Study 3: Dance Music

Section Five — Area of Study 4: Traditions and Innovation

Section Six — Bonus Track

Section Seven — Glossary and Index

Published by Coordination Group Publications Ltd.

Main Author:
Elena Delaney

Further Contributors:
Martin Chester
Taissa Csáky
Matthew Delaney
Tim Major
Katherine Reed
Claire Thompson

With thanks to Glenn Rogers, Janice Baiton and Jacqueline Brockway for the proofreading.

ISBN-10: 1 84146 788 X
ISBN-13: 978 1 84146 788 7

Groovy website: www.cgpbooks.co.uk

Jolly bits of clipart from CorelDRAW®

Printed by Elanders Hindson Ltd, Newcastle upon Tyne

What You Have to Do for GCSE Music

Music GCSE doesn't cover every single aspect of music — if it did it would take forever.
Instead you focus on four main 'Areas of Study' (AoS for short).

You Learn About Four Topics

> **AoS1 — EXPLOITING THE RESOURCE** *(covered in Section 2)*
> For this one you study <u>your</u> instrument or voice.

> **AoS2 — TECHNIQUES OF MELODIC COMPOSITION** *(see Section 3)*
> For Area of Study 2 you learn about different ways of writing melodies.

> **AoS3 — DANCE MUSIC** *(covered in Section 4)*
> In this Area of Study you learn about three different styles of dance music
> — Elizabethan dances called the pavan and galliard, waltzes and disco.

> **AoS4 — TRADITIONS AND INNOVATION** *(see Section 5)*
> This one's about the way composers combine old and new ideas. You look at
> three different types of music that do this — bhangra, salsa and minimalism.

*The Areas of Study were
first discovered in 1483.*

You do a Mixture of Coursework...

The coursework is work done during the course. Obviously. It's split into two chunks.

PART A — INTEGRATED COURSEWORK

worth <u>35%</u> of the total marks

This bit of the coursework covers *AoS1, Exploiting the Resource* — you study
<u>three</u> pieces of music for your instrument or voice and do work based on all three.

1) You <u>perform</u> one of the pieces and write an <u>appraisal</u> to say how well you think you
   played and what you could have done better.
2) You <u>compose</u> a new piece using ideas from all three pieces. Before you start
   composing you write a <u>brief</u> saying what you're planning to do. Afterwards you write
   an <u>appraisal</u>, saying how well you think you followed the brief.

PART B — FURTHER COURSEWORK

worth <u>25%</u> of the total marks

1) You <u>perform</u> another piece — this can be anything you like.
2) You <u>compose</u> one more piece, in one of the styles covered in *AoS3* and *4*.

...and Exams

At the end of Year 11 you do <u>two exams</u>.

1) <u>TERMINAL TASK</u> — you have to <u>compose</u> a piece of music using what you learned in *AoS2*.
   On this paper you can pick up <u>15%</u> of the marks available.
2) <u>LISTENING AND APPRAISING</u> — you <u>listen</u> to music from *AoS2, 3* and *4* and <u>answer questions</u> on it.
   This paper's worth <u>25%</u> of the overall mark.

Err, Miss... is it too late to change to physics?

Welcome to the wonderful world of GCSE Music. Breathe in the cool clear air. Listen to the birds.
It's so beautiful, I could cry. Well actually, I couldn't, but it's <u>OK</u> compared to some subjects.

Coursework — Performance

You do two performances altogether — one for the integrated coursework, and one for the further bit. The better you play, the more marks you get — so pick 'em carefully and practise hard.

You Have to Do Two Performances

1) The piece you play for Performance 1 has to be one of the three you're studying for *AoS1* (*integrated coursework*).
2) The piece you play for Performances 2 can be anything you like.
3) One of the two performances has to be a solo (though it's OK to have a simple accompaniment).
4) The other piece has to be an ensemble piece — anything from a duet to a full band, so long as you have an important part (playing third triangle in a full symphony orchestra won't quite cut it, I'm afraid).

> So, say you play the violin — you could do a violin duet for Performance 1
> and a solo with piano accompaniment for Performance 2.

There Are Up to Ten Marks for the Quality of your Playing

For each performance, you can get up to ten marks for 'musicality'. You get marks for —

1) *CONFIDENCE* You can't play confidently unless you know your piece inside out.
   A few nerves are normal, but they won't spoil your performance if you're really well prepared.
2) *FLUENCY* Lots of stopping and starting or slowing down for tricky bits will lose you marks. Keep going.
3) *TECHNICAL CONTROL* This means your physical ability to play or sing the piece.
4) *MUSICAL EXPRESSION* Your performance needs to make the audience feel something. Pay attention to stuff like dynamics, tempo, mood, articulation and phrasing. If they're not written in, work out your own.
5) *ENSEMBLE SKILLS* Obviously you only get marks for this when you're playing in an ensemble. Play in time with the other players. Really listen to the other parts, so you know when you should be part of the background and when you should make your part stand out.

There Are Up to Five Marks for the Difficulty of the Piece

A really simple piece, in an easy key like C major, with easy rhythms (say just crotchets and quavers) and small straightforward jumps between notes, will get no marks or maybe one mark for difficulty.

A piece of music in a tricky key with lots of sharps and flats, which is very fast or has complicated rhythms and difficult leaps between notes could get four or five marks for difficulty.

> **CHOOSE YOUR PIECES CAREFULLY**
>
> 1) Ideally they should be the hardest level that you can play well.
> 2) If you pick something too easy, you'll be throwing away difficulty marks.
> 3) If you pick something too hard, you won't be able to play your best, and you'll be throwing away marks for musicality.
> 4) Get your music teacher or instrument teacher's advice on what to play.

Practise, Practise, Scales, Practise, Every Day, Practise...

Hmmm... How am I going to get you to take this in...
No doubt people have been going on at you about practising since you were knee-high to a piccolo...
The more my music teachers went on at me about practising, the less I felt like doing it...
I expect you know that you need to do lots of practice. So we'll just leave it there.

Appraising Your Performance

After you've done <u>Performance 1</u>, you have to write an <u>appraisal</u> — an essay on how well you think you played. Here's an example of an appraisal — try and cover all these topics in yours.

Give Details About the Piece You Played

1) Write about the BACKGROUND.

2) Mention the STYLE.

3) Say how the MOOD is created.

4) Say how the piece uses the RANGE and TIMBRE of your instrument.

5) Mention any special ways the piece uses TECHNIQUES or STYLES specific to your instrument.

6) Say how your part relates to OTHER PERFORMERS' PARTS.

For my performance I played the popular Beatles song *Eleanor Rigby*, arranged for clarinet with piano accompaniment. The arrangement includes three variations on the original tune. The original pop style of the piece comes through in the syncopated rhythms, simple ostinato style accompaniment and AB structure of the main theme.

The lyrics of the original song talk about 'all the lonely people' and this arrangement has the same sad, empty feeling. The mood is set by: the minor key (E minor transposed to F sharp minor for the clarinet part); the moderate tempo (♩=138); and the use of the rich, melancholy timbre of the clarinet's lower register. This piece uses nearly the whole of the clarinet's wide range, which gives lots of contrasting timbres across the low, middle and high registers.

The piece moves gradually higher and louder (*mf*) through each variation. In variation 3 it returns to the lowest and softest (*pp*) notes. This gives an overall arch shape to the piece and highlights the wide dynamic range of the clarinet. Contrasts of articulation — staccato, accents and legato — are used. For example the theme is played all slurred whereas Variation 2 has a real mixture of wide leaps, accents and slurs. These contrasts and the wide leaps gave me an opportunity to demonstrate my technical abilities. Variations 2 and 3 also gave me the opportunity to demonstrate two characteristic styles of clarinet playing: variation 2 uses jazzy swinging quavers, whereas variation 3 is written in a stricter classical style.

The piano part is the same for each variation. It never has the tune, but the piano supplies the bass line and some important harmonies. It also adds to the syncopated rhythmic feel, particularly where the rocking crotchet ostinato moves from the strong beats to the weak beats in bars 9-10 and 15-17.

Compare it to the Other Two Pieces

The other pieces that I studied — the fourth movement of Mozart's *Clarinet Quintet* and Theme and Variation I and XII from *An Elgar Clarinet Album* are written in the same variation form and arranged with piano accompaniment, but are quite different in their mood and style. The Mozart has a faster, livelier mood and tempo and the Elgar is slower and more relaxed. Like *Eleanor Rigby*, the other pieces use lots of contrasting articulation for the clarinet. However, both have more detailed performance directions: the tempo and rhythm in particular is varied with ritardandos, rallentandos and pauses and a much wider range of dynamics is used.

Eleanor Rigby has less detailed performance directions because it was written for pop performers who expect to improvise. The classical pieces have more precise directions as the composers had a more precise result in mind. The Mozart piece also shows its classical origins in the use of ornamentation — mainly trills which were popular in the Classical period.

The Mozart and Elgar both have sections where the piano has the melody, for example, in the Mozart the clarinet plays Alberti bass chord patterns at some points to accompany the piano. This is because both pieces were originally written for larger groups of musicians where the clarinet did not have the tune all the time. *Eleanor Rigby* was written for a pop band where the lead singer has the tune all the time — the clarinet part reproduces the part of the lead singer.

1) Talk about the OTHER PIECES you studied for AoS1. Mention similarities and differences to the piece you performed.

2) Compare the way the DATE the pieces were composed affects the COMPOSITION and NOTATION.

3) Write about the way your instrument relates to OTHER PERFORMERS in the other pieces you studied.

Evaluate Your Performance

1) Say WHAT WENT WELL.

Overall, I was pleased with my performance. In rehearsals, I was worried about coming in on time for each new variation but I watched the pianist carefully and we managed to come in together neatly, which was very satisfying. I was also pleased that my high register notes sounded clear and didn't squeak. I think the fact that I followed all the composer's dynamic markings made the piece sound more musical.

2) Say WHAT YOU COULD HAVE DONE BETTER.

My articulation should have been better in Variation 2, where I lost concentration. For a future performance, I would spend more time practising the composer's exact tonguing and slurring directions.

Composition — The Brief

There are three parts to writing your GCSE coursework compositions — the brief, the actual composition and an appraisal. All three bits are important. Don't go skimping any of them.

You Have to Write Two Compositions for Your Coursework

1) Composition 1 has to be for your instrument — it has to link to the three pieces you've studied for AoS1, Exploiting The Resource.

2) Composition 2 has to be in one of the styles you've learned about in AoS3 and 4 — a pavan/galliard, waltz or disco tune, or something in bhangra, salsa or minimalist style. Composition 2 can be an arrangement — but you only get marks for the ways you change the original, so it's not a soft option.

The Brief Says What Your Plans Are

A brief is a write-up of your ideas for your composition. It might seem like a bit of a pain to spend time writing the brief when you could be getting on with composing, but if you do it well, it should make tackling the composition loads easier because it gives you a starting point.

The brief should cover all of these things:

1) The type of piece you're going to compose, e.g. a waltz.
2) The instruments you're planning to use.
3) The musical techniques and ideas that you intend to use.
4) Clear details of how your composition links to AoS 1, 3 or 4.

Here's an example brief for a Composition 2 piece. It mentions:

instruments and equipment →

the style →

the main idea →

techniques and details that are typical of the chosen style

Composition 2
Resources: Percussion ensemble (various instruments) and voices (two male and two female). Work will be composed on a sequencer. Voice parts will either be recorded or performed live against the sequenced backing track.
Focus for study: Minimalist music

Brief
To compose a piece of atmospheric music for percussion ensemble and voices that represents a factory, two minutes before shut down.
• Use minimalist techniques to create an atmosphere of working machinery. Use different length ostinato patterns to represent various machines, layering patterns to give the impression of more than one machine working at once.
• Gradually change the ostinati, e.g. by using additive melody over time to represent the slowing down of certain machines; start with more complicated rhythms and gradually simplify.
• Over the top of this background music use voices to sing short, repeated melodies and word phrases (call and response patterns) to set the atmosphere, e.g. machines closing down as a contrast with people getting excited about finishing work.

Both Briefs are Important

The brief for Composition 1 is part of your coursework. You get marks for it — they're testing how good you are at communicating your ideas.

The brief for Composition 2 isn't marked, but that doesn't mean it's not important. It needs to be clear and detailed so the examiners can mark your composition properly. The brief for Composition 2 goes on the Candidate's Intention Form along with your appraisal. You can hand your appraisal in as a recording if you prefer that to writing it down.

Writing Your Composition

Well, the good news is, none of the compositions you have to do for GCSE is <u>allowed</u> to be more than <u>three minutes</u> long. So no one's expecting you to write an opera. Something short will do it.

Try and Stick to Your Brief

1) <u>Ideally</u> you'll be able to just sit down and compose your piece with no problems. In the <u>real world</u> things don't always work out as you expect. You may find that your plans for a <u>saxophone septet</u> won't work out because all seven of your saxophone-playing cousins are leaving town.

Man, I love this crazy salsa beat.

2) If you <u>have</u> to change your plans, stick to the same <u>style</u> of music. If you originally planned to write a <u>salsa piece</u> for seven saxophones, you <u>can</u> switch to a <u>salsa piece</u> for solo glockenspiel. You <u>can't</u> switch to a bhangra-style piece for solo glockenspiel. If you change the <u>style</u> you'll lose <u>a stack of marks</u>.

3) If your composition ends up being different from what you described in the brief, say <u>what you changed</u> and <u>why you changed it</u> on the <u>Candidate's Intentions Form</u> for Composition 2, or in the <u>appraisal</u> for Composition 1.

4) Try and stick to your brief though. If you keep changing your plans you could find you <u>never</u> end up with a finished piece.

Make Sure Each Piece Uses the Right Techniques

The examiners don't just want to see whether you can compose <u>any old piece of music</u>. Oh no. For Composition 1 they want to see that you can compose a piece that <u>relates to the other pieces you've studied</u>. For Composition 2 they want to see that you can compose a piece <u>in a certain style</u>.

For <u>Composition 1</u> make a list of the different techniques (e.g. ostinato, legato, walking bass) used in the <u>three pieces</u> you're studying. For <u>Composition 2</u>, once you've decided on the style of music you want to compose in, find the right section in this book and make a list of the techniques used <u>in that style</u>.

When you're <u>writing</u> your compositions, <u>check</u> the techniques you're using against the ones in your lists.

You Need to Decide How to Hand In Your Work

You can hand in your completed composition as a <u>recording</u>, a <u>written version</u> or <u>both</u>. If you hand in both versions, tell the examiners which one is the <u>definitive version</u> — the one which is most like what you hoped to achieve.

WRITTEN VERSIONS
1) These can be in...
   • <u>standard</u> notation, i.e. on a stave
   • <u>graphic</u> notation, i.e. in symbols
   • a <u>computer</u> score
   • <u>melody lines</u> and/or lyrics and chord charts
2) Give as much <u>information</u> as possible. Details of <u>dynamics</u>, <u>tempo</u>, <u>expression</u> and <u>articulation</u> will all improve your mark.

RECORDINGS
1) You don't get any marks for recording quality, but <u>good recordings</u> are <u>easier</u> to mark.
2) If you've had help from your teacher with equipment like sequencers — <u>say so</u> in your appraisal.
3) You also need to mention it in your appraisal if your composition includes material from sources like <u>MIDI files</u> or <u>samples</u> from the Internet.

Even if you decide against handing in a recording, <u>listen</u> to what you've written before you hand it in. Get some mates to <u>play</u> the piece for you, or <u>record</u> it so you can sit back and concentrate on listening.

I bet Beethoven never had to write a brief...

On the one hand, you've got almost <u>two years</u> to get these compositions sorted. On the other hand, if you don't start ASAP you might just find yourself <u>running out of time</u>. Best <u>get on with it</u>.

Composition — The Appraisal

Not content with making you <u>sweat</u>, <u>struggle</u> and <u>toil</u> over your composition, the examiners now expect you to write an <u>appraisal</u> for it. What more do they want... blood...

The Appraisal is Your Assessment of the Composition

An appraisal is a <u>detailed description</u> of the way you <u>put your composition together</u> and what you think of the <u>results</u>. You won't get away with saying your piece is "quite good" or "not as good as I'd hoped".

... likewise don't write a novel about it.

To make sure your appraisal goes into enough detail, try answering <u>each of these questions</u>:

* How <u>similar</u> is the composition to what you described in the brief?
* Did you <u>change</u> any of your original ideas as you went along? Why?
* Which are the <u>most successful</u> bits of your composition?
* Which bits are <u>less successful</u>? What would you like to <u>improve</u>?
* When you were composing the piece, was there anything you found <u>difficult</u>?
* When you tried out your piece did it sound how you <u>expected</u> it to? What was different?

FOR COMPOSITION 1:
* How do the musical ideas and techniques <u>relate to</u> the three pieces you studied for AoS1?

FOR COMPOSITION 2:
* What musical ideas and techniques from your composition belong to the musical <u>style</u> you're writing in?

<u>Don't forget</u> you have to mention all of this stuff too:

* *Any technical help you had with recording*
* *Any changes from the brief*
* *Any bits like MIDI files that you've sampled*
* *If you've done a written version and a recording, which one's closest to what you originally planned?*

Composition 1 and Composition 2 Appraisals are Different

The appraisal for <u>Composition 1</u> is part and parcel of the '<u>integrated coursework</u>' — that means it's worth <u>marks</u> and it's worth making it <u>detailed</u>. Like the brief for Composition 1 you can hand your appraisal in as a <u>recording</u> if you prefer that to writing it down.

The appraisal for Composition 2 is <u>a bit different</u> from the one for Composition 1. You write it on the Candidate's Intention Form along with your brief. It <u>isn't marked</u> but the examiners <u>will</u> see it. If it's good, and you explain your thoughts about your composition clearly, it could still help you get better marks for the <u>composition</u>.

Next they'll be asking for an appraisal of the appraisal...

Even if you do an outstanding, extraordinary, unbelievably brilliant composition, a rough, sketchy, slapdash appraisal will <u>let you down</u>. Big time. Don't forget the appraisal's <u>part of the project</u>.

The Listening Exam

When all the coursework's done and handed in, you can just sit back, stick a CD on and relax, can't you...
OH NO YOU CAN'T — you've got to do a listening exam. All 90 minutes of it. Whoopee-doodle-DOO.

The Listening Exam Tests AoS2, 3 and 4

1) The Listening Exam is worth 25% of your total mark — that's a big chunk of marks.

2) As you might have guessed, it involves listening. The invigilator plays music from a CD.
You listen to the music and answer written questions about it.

3) There are lots of bits of music to listen to. Each one has its own set of questions. You'll hear
a piece three or four times and do all the questions for it before moving on to the next one.

4) Concentrate on answering just a few of questions each time the music's played — it's less confusing.

5) You don't get a lot of time on this paper — think fast and write fast.

6) Each group of questions is marked with the AoS number at the beginning.
Make sure you know which AoS is which — they're all on P.1.

Some Questions are Multiple Choice

OK, you can't hang around on this paper, but don't botch this bit by rushing — read all the options carefully.

 What type of scale is used for this melody? Underline your answer.

Whole tone   **Major**   **Raga**   **Modal**

If you get stuck — guess the answer. There's a 25% chance of getting it right.

Some Questions Just Need a Short Answer

These questions test your detailed knowledge of the AoS. They're only worth a couple of marks
so don't waste time writing your answer out in a nice long sentence — just stick it down.

 Apart from the rhythm, what other elements of this
music are influenced by African music? (2 marks)

Sometimes They Give You an Outline of the Music

You could get an outline of part of the music called a 'skeleton score'. It will just show part of the music —
the melody, rhythm or lyrics, say. The skeleton score will help you with answering the question.

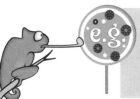 On the Extract Sheet is a skeleton score of a melody
that you will hear **four** times.

Describe the melodic movement in bar 5.
Refer to overall shape, steps and leaps,
harmony and phrasing. (5 marks)

Questions Worth Four or Five Marks Need a Longer Answer

These are questions where you have to write a longer answer — either lists of words and phrases, or a
couple of paragraphs of continuous writing. To work out how much to write, look at the number of marks.

 Compare the two extracts in as much detail as you can. Comment on tempo,
melody, harmony, dynamics and the way the composer uses the orchestra. (5 marks)

Arrrr, shiver me timbers — 'tis the skeleton score...

If you think of an answer while the CD's playing, just use a pencil and scribble it down. After each
question the music stops to give you writing time — use that time to write the answer neatly in pen.

The Terminal Task

The Terminal Task tests you on *AoS2 — Techniques of Melodic Composition*. Or to put it another way, you have to compose a piece of music in 30 minutes flat. Scary or what...

You Get a Choice of Ideas to Get You Started

1) Before you start on the Terminal Task, you'll get a piece of paper showing a <u>rhythmic</u> idea, a <u>pattern of notes</u> and a <u>chord pattern</u>. These starting points are sometimes called the 'stimuli'.

2) You could get something like this —

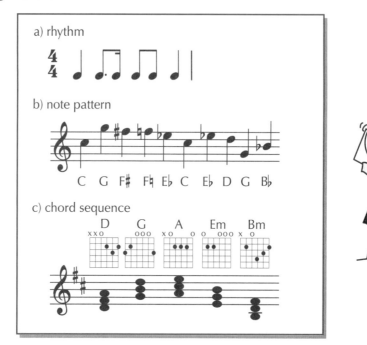

3) Your teacher will also <u>play</u> you <u>each stimulus</u>.
4) When you've heard them all once you have to choose <u>one</u> to base your composition on.
5) Once you've chosen which stimulus you're going to use, your teacher's allowed to play it to you <u>twice more</u>. You can <u>record</u> the stimulus to help you when you're composing.

You Get 25 Minutes to Compose Your Piece

1) You get <u>25 minutes</u> to compose your piece.
2) That's <u>not long</u> so work in the way that <u>suits you</u> best.
3) You can <u>record</u> your composition as you go along — on <u>tape</u>, <u>computer</u> or <u>paper</u>.

- improvise and develop your ideas using an instrument or your voice
- write your ideas down on paper
- use computers or other music technology

You Get 5 Minutes to Present Your Composition

At the end of the preparation time you have <u>5 minutes</u> to present your work.
You can do this is one of three ways —

1) Play it <u>live</u>.
2) Play it back through a <u>sequencer</u> or other recording device, like a <u>tape recorder</u>.
3) Spend the 5 minutes polishing up your <u>written version</u> and hand it in.

The Terminal Task

Make Some Quick Decisions to Get Started

Once you've picked your stimulus, you're <u>stuck with it</u>. Now you've got
to decide a couple of really important things so you can get started:

1) If you've chosen the rhythm pattern stimulus, you need a <u>scale</u> for your melody. It can be <u>major</u>, <u>minor</u>, <u>modal</u>, <u>blues</u>, <u>pentatonic</u> or <u>whole tone</u>. These are all covered in *AoS2* (Section 3 of this book) and in the Core book (also Section 3, oddly).

2) It's way easier to do the composition if you decide on your <u>structure</u> before you start. The most obvious choices are tried-and-tested plans like <u>binary</u>, <u>ternary</u>, <u>rondo</u> or variations (pages 18–19).

Here's a Melody I Prepared Earlier...

In case you're not too sure how to turn a 'stimulus' into music, here's a melody based on <u>stimulus a)</u> from the page opposite. The notes of Section A are taken from a C major pentatonic scale — CDEGA. The notes of Section B are taken from the G major pentatonic — GABDE.
Follow them through a bar at a time to see what I've done.

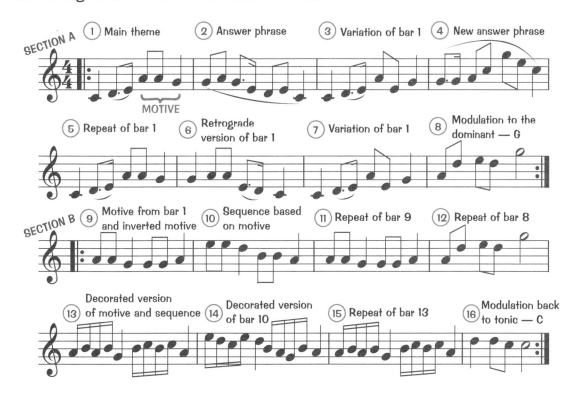

Make Sure Your Piece is Expressive

1) Once you've got your tune make sure it's <u>expressive</u>.

2) If you're handing it in <u>in writing</u>, add in <u>dynamics</u>, <u>tempo</u>, <u>phrasing</u> and <u>articulation</u>.

3) If you're presenting your piece by <u>performing it</u>, make sure your playing or singing has all the louds and softs, and other things it needs to sound as good as it can.

4) <u>Don't</u> wait till the last minute to think about this stuff — bear it in mind as you're composing.

Terminal 1 for Europe and Africa — Terminal Task for Hell...*

AoS2 is all about <u>Melodic</u> Composition — it's the <u>tune</u> you need to concentrate on. You don't need a harmony or fantastically fancy rhythms. Just write a <u>good melody</u> with a <u>solid structure</u>.

* ...which is actually a small town in Norway, just north of Trondheim. In case you're interested.

Getting to Know Your Instrument *

For <u>AoS1</u> you study your <u>voice or instrument</u> by learning 3 pieces for it. Then you <u>show you know your stuff</u> through the integrated coursework — a performance and a composition. Here's what you need to learn...

'Exploiting the Resource' is All Coursework

All you actually <u>hand in</u> for AoS1 is <u>Performance 1</u> (+Appraisal) and <u>Composition 1</u> (+Brief+Appraisal). *BUT...* that's <u>not all</u> the work you have to <u>do</u>.

<u>First</u> you've got to <u>choose three pieces</u> to study (get teach's help with this), <u>then</u> you've got to <u>learn them</u> really well. <u>At the same time</u> you've got to learn <u>all about your voice or instrument</u> *(that's this section of the book)*. You <u>won't</u> be able to do a decent job of the performance and composition unless you've done <u>all that</u>.

Get to Know Your Instrument Inside Out

Find out as much as you can on your voice or instrument — talk to <u>other players</u> and your <u>teachers</u>, look at <u>books</u> and listen to lots of <u>music</u>. Make yourself into a total violin/clarinet/guitar/didgeridoo <u>geek</u>.

You should <u>at least</u> know —

- *the <u>range</u> of your instrument — the highest and lowest notes it can play (see P.13 for the ranges of some popular instruments)*

- *the <u>timbre</u> of your instrument — whether it makes a woody, soft, mellow, reedy, tinkly or sweet sound*

- *how the timbre <u>changes</u> in <u>different registers</u>, e.g. a violin is mellow in lower registers and shriller in higher registers*

- *what type of <u>ensemble</u> (orchestra, rock band, brass band...) your instrument's usually played in*

- *whether your instrument works <u>acoustically</u>, or needs <u>amplification</u>*

Work Out How Your Instrument Fits Into Its Family

Instruments are grouped into general <u>families</u>. It'll help you understand more about your instrument and how it's <u>used</u> if you know what family it's from.

These are the <u>four main families</u> of instruments —

WOODWIND e.g. flute, clarinet, saxophone, oboe, bassoon	*BRASS* e.g. trumpet, cornet, horn, trombone, tuba
STRINGS violin, viola, cello, double bass, harp, guitar	*PERCUSSION* tuned (e.g. glockenspiel or xylophone), untuned (e.g. snare drum or cymbals)

Not forgetting, of course, the old joanna. The piano's a weird one. It's a percussion instrument because it has hammers, but it's also a string instrument because it's got strings. As far as I know, the jury's still out on that one.

Once you know what family your instrument's from, work out <u>how it fits in</u> —

- *Is it <u>higher</u> or <u>lower</u> than others in the group?*

- *Does it <u>produce sound</u> the same way as others in the group, or is there something different about it? e.g. within the brass family, a trumpet uses valves, but a trombone has a slide.*

- *Are there other <u>similar instruments</u> to yours? E.g. there are tenor, alto and soprano saxophones.*

_Composing for Your Instrument_*

Almost all instruments can do something that other instruments can't. You may as well make the most of that — a) because you _can_, and b) because it'll get you more marks. Bonus.

Play to Your Strengths

Try and use at least a couple of the 'strengths' of your instrument or its family in your composition:

WOODWIND
* contrasting articulation — slurring and tonguing
* contrast in timbre between different registers
* with flutes you can do 'flutter tonguing' by making an 'r' sound as you blow
* for more modern-sounding pieces — key rattling and blowing air without producing notes

---

BRASS
* can put mutes in the bell to change the tone
* can do double- and triple-tonguing
* trombones can play _glissandi_ — sounds made by moving the slide quickly up or down
* can rattle the valves and blow without making a note, just like woodwind

---

STRINGS
* pizzicato — plucking the strings with fingers
* tremolo — moving the bow up and down really fast
* _sul ponticello_ — bowing right by the bridge to get a screechy, spooky sound
* mutes make the timbre softer and thinner (_con sordini_ means with mute, _senza sordini_ means without it)
* down bows (marked ⌐) sound stronger than up bows (marked ∨)

PERCUSSION
* biggest strength is the number and variety of different instruments — e.g. a drumkit could have everything from a bass drum to cowbells
* different sticks, mallets and brushes change the sound of percussion instruments
* drum rolls can be performed on most percussion — they're _[cue drum roll]_ great

---

PIANO
* can use right-hand pedal to sustain notes (℘⒟. means press the pedal, ✳ means release it)
* can mute notes with the left-hand pedal
* can play up to 10 notes at once without pedal (and loads if you use the right-hand pedal)
* one person can play both melody and accompaniment, or even two independent parts

---

Remember — Instruments and Voices Have Limits

Some people get carried away when they're composing, asking instruments and singers to do things that are just about impossible. Don't be mean. Be a nice composer.

1) Leave breathing space for woodwind and brass players.
2) If there are mute passages, give the players time to put on or take off their mutes.
3) Don't write impossible dynamics — some instruments have trouble controlling dynamics in certain registers. (e.g. the lowest register of an oboe is really loud, so you shouldn't write low-pitched quiet bits for oboes)
4) Don't write impossible notes — stick to the range of the instrument or singer you're composing for.
5) Transpose parts for transposing instruments (see P.12).
6) Don't assume C major is the easiest key to play. Find out the easiest key for your instrument.

To know your instrument is to love it — or so they say...

Face it, your instrument is different. It's special. It's beautiful. Think like that — and _compose_ like that — and the examiners will love you. (...well, give you better marks anyway — which is probably better, to be honest)

Transposing Instruments

Transposing — what a pain... If musicians had sat down and had a <u>sensible chat</u> a few hundred years ago, I'm sure we could have <u>avoided</u> transposing somehow. But we're <u>stuck</u> with it now.

The Notes Sounded are Different from the Notes Written

Transposing instruments are mostly <u>brass</u> and <u>woodwind</u>. The notes they <u>play</u> come out <u>higher</u> or <u>lower</u> than the notes <u>written</u> in the music. E.g. when a clarinetist plays a C from the clarinet part, it comes out as <u>B♭</u>.

This is <u>just a tad confusing</u>. I'll put it another way:

> If you play a transposing instrument you probably know a bit about transposing already. If you don't, you need to learn, so you know what's going on when you <u>play with</u> or <u>write for</u> transposing instruments.

1) Nice, ordinary instruments like violins and pianos are <u>tuned</u> to the <u>key of C</u>. This is called <u>concert pitch</u>.

2) <u>Transposing instruments</u> are tuned to <u>different keys</u>.
   (e.g. clarinets are tuned to B♭ and alto saxophones are tuned to E♭)

3) Music for transposing instruments has to be written out a bit <u>higher</u> or <u>lower</u> than it would be for instruments that don't transpose. It needs a <u>different key signature</u> too, so the intervals stay the same.

EXAMPLE:

> Transposing instruments in <u>B♭</u> sound <u>one tone lower</u> than concert pitch.
> *To get them to play a concert pitch C you have to write <u>D</u>. All the notes in the written part <u>look</u> one tone higher than they <u>sound</u>.*

This is the melody a violin might play — it's in C major.

> Transposing instruments in <u>E♭</u> sound a <u>minor third higher</u> than concert pitch.
> *To get them to play a concert pitch C you have to write an <u>A</u>. All the notes in the written part <u>look</u> a minor third lower than they <u>sound</u>.*

This is the same melody transposed for a B♭ clarinet. It's in D major but the notes will be the same as the violin.

This is the same melody transposed for my dad. It's in D major, but he'll sing it in F♯ minor, get all the notes wrong and maybe end up somewhere near what the violin was originally playing.

These are the Most Common Transposing Instruments

These are the transposing instruments you're <u>most likely</u> to come across:

In B♭...   clarinet, tenor saxophone, trumpet and cornet

In F...   French horn   **In E♭...**   alto saxophone, tenor horn

Some transposing instruments are <u>tuned to concert pitch</u> but play notes an <u>octave higher</u> than they are written, e.g. the <u>piccolo</u>. Likewise, some are <u>tuned to concert pitch</u> but play notes an <u>octave lower</u> than they are written, e.g. the <u>double bass</u>.

For Mixed Ensembles Write First, Transpose Later

1) If you're composing for an <u>ensemble</u> with concert pitch instruments <u>and</u> transposing instruments, write <u>all the parts</u> at <u>concert pitch</u> first, then transpose the ones that need transposing after.

2) If you've got <u>sequencing software</u>, that makes life even easier, because you can get the <u>computer</u> to do the transposing for you.

Transposing — a load of cross-dressers showing off...

Transposing is <u>meant</u> to make life <u>easier</u> for musicians. It makes the players' jobs easier, but I'm not sure it makes life easier for composers. In fact, this is quite possibly one of the <u>hardest</u>, <u>most confusing</u>, <u>most mind-frying</u> pages in the book. There's no way you understood first time round. Go back and <u>read it again</u>.

Ranges for Voices and Instruments

This page may not look <u>exciting</u> but it is <u>useful</u> — when you're composing, check the range of each instrument here, to make sure it's actually possible to play what you've written.

Woodwind Instruments

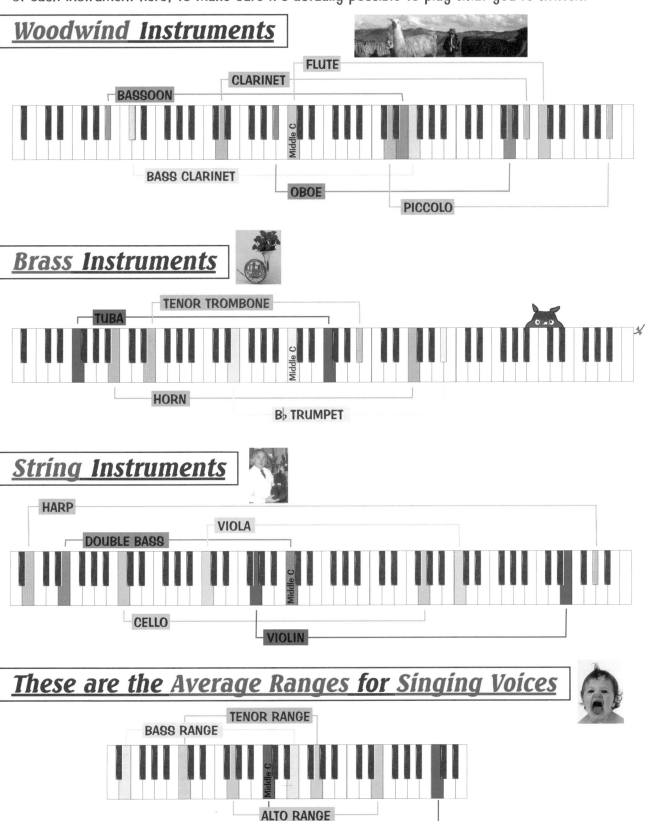

Brass Instruments

String Instruments

These are the Average Ranges for Singing Voices

Give me a home where the buffalo roam...

Don't let these diagrams give you a headache. If you're super-dweeby keen, you could memorise them all so you don't need to look anything up. But I wouldn't bother. I'd just use them <u>for reference</u>.

Melody

For Area of Study 2 you learn all about how different types of melody are put together. They test this in the Listening Test and *(shudder)* the Terminal Task. Learn the jargon on this page to help you through Listening.

Melody = Tune

I don't want to patronise anyone here. I mean, you know what a melody is — it's the tune. But just to be on the safe side here's the official definition of a melody.

A MELODY IS a series of notes with:
1) notes at different pitches — some higher, some lower
2) a rhythm

In the Listening test you have to write about how the melodies you hear are put together. The main things they'll ask about are scale, contour, range, phrasing and structure.

The Notes of a Melody are from a Scale

The notes in a melody aren't just random — they almost all come from one scale. There are all sorts of scale — major, minor, modal... and more. Each one has its own special sound. Make a point of learning how different scales sound, so you can spot them in the exam.

The Contour is how the Pitch Changes

1) The notes can step up or down to the next note. A melody with lots of step movements is called scalic.
2) There can be a big leap between one note and the next.
3) The melody can go through the notes of a chord.
4) Notes can be repeated.

A Melody can have a Wide Range or a Narrow Range

The range is the gap between the top and bottom notes of a melody.
If the melody you're listening to has really high notes and really low notes it's got a wide range.
If the bottom and top notes aren't that far apart, it's got a narrow range.

Melodies Divide Up into Phrases and Sections

In any melody you'll hear groups of bars that feel as if they belong together. These are the phrases.
1) Phrases in a tune usually have an even number of bars — most often four.
2) Phrases sometimes start on a weak beat (called an anacrusis) usually the last beat of the bar. All the other phrases in the melody will start with an anacrusis too.
3) In the Listening exam you could get asked whether the melody in a phrase is new, repeated or varied.

A group of phrases makes a longer bit of tune called a section. The way these sections are put together gives music its overall shape, or structure. Some structures, like binary, ternary, rondo and variation form are quite formal — they've been used by lots of composers over the years and there are rules about how they work. There's more about these on P.18 and 19.

On a scale of 1–10 where would you put GCSE Music...

That's the basics. The rest of this section's all about different ways melodies have been put together over the years. Maybe I should make it sound more exciting — HERE COMES THE FASCINATING STORY OF MELODY! IN TECHNICOLOR! AND DOLBY SURROUND SOUND! STARRING GEORGE CLOONEY! Yup, that's better.

Modal Melody — Plainchant

Plainchant is as old as the hills. Well, not quite that old, actually. But it's really, really old.

Plainchant Melodies were Sung in Church

1) Plainchants were written by monks for singing in their monastery church.

2) The words are Latin religious texts, sung as part of the Mass (church service).

3) Plainchant is the oldest written music there is. Most plainchants were written in the Middle Ages — 800ish to 1500ish.

4) Some people call plainchant 'plainsong' or 'Gregorian chant'. They're talking about the same type of music.

Plainchant is Unaccompanied with No Fixed Rhythm

Plainchant is traditionally sung by an all-male choir. (Well, there weren't any women in the monasteries.) It sounds best in big stone churches or cathedrals — just like the places where it was originally performed. It has a very pure, clear sound.

1) There's no accompaniment — no organ, no orchestra, just voices.

2) All the voices sing in unison — everybody sings the same notes. The posh name for music with a single line of melody is monophonic. Remember that word — 'monophonic' — the examiners will like it.

3) The contour of the melody moves mainly by step, with maybe one leap in each phrase.

4) Plainchant has free metre — there's no time signature at the beginning of the music and none of the notes has a stem to tell you how long it is. The music gets its rhythm from the natural stresses of the words.

5) For variety, the melody in some plainchant is passed between different groups of voices. In antiphony the melody passes between two choirs at opposite ends of the church. In call and response the melody is passed between a soloist/small group and the full choir.

Plainchant is Modal

Plainchant sounds nothing like classical music or modern pop. Partly that's because of the choir and free-flowing rhythm. Another big reason is that the notes come from modes. Up until about 1600 most music in Europe was written using modes.

MODES

1) Modes are sets of eight notes that start and end on the same letter, just like modern major and minor scales. Modes can be formed by playing a major scale starting on, say, the second or third note (or whatever).

2) E.g. if you play D to D on a piano, using only the white notes, you're playing in the Dorian mode. E to E would be in the Phrygian mode. There are loads of them, but you don't need to know all their names — just remember they exist.

3) Modern major and minor scales have a semitone gap between Note 7 and Note 8, whereas modes often have a whole tone gap. Note 7 is really important in giving music its flavour, so this makes a big difference to the sound of modal music.

MODES IN PLAINCHANT

1) Plainchant melodies are written within the range of a set mode, e.g. a plainchant in the Dorian mode in D would only contain the notes D, E, F, G, A, B, C.

2) Whatever note a plainchant is based on (e.g. it might start or end on D or have key phrases that revolve around D) is called the final. In the example above, the pitch D would be the final wherever it appeared in the plainchant.

I really feel like a pizza...

Spotting a plainchant is about as difficult as spotting an elephant in a supermarket. It's really distinctive. As always in music, a CD is worth 1000 words. Have a listen to some plainchant, to see what it's like.

Pentatonic Melody — British Folk Music

Even if you think you don't know anything about folk music you probably do. You've probably heard drunks singing <u>Auld Lang Syne</u> at New Year, or had to do <u>country dancing</u> at primary school — it's *that* kind of music.

Folk Music was Played by Ordinary People

1) Folk music's still around nowadays but it used to be <u>much more popular</u>. In olden times, before radios and record players, the <u>only</u> music ordinary people had was music they played themselves.

2) The tunes tend to be quite <u>simple</u> and work with just a <u>few</u> instruments or voices. This made them easier for Jo Bloggs in the pub, or field, or factory, to learn and play.

3) Folk music was hardly ever written down. It survived through the <u>oral tradition</u> — people heard a song or tune they liked and <u>memorised</u> it.

4) Folk music changes over time as people add <u>new ideas</u>. Sometimes they're being deliberately <u>creative</u>, sometimes they <u>can't remember</u> exactly what they've heard and make up a new bit to fill the gap.

5) The instruments used to play along with folk songs and dances tend to be <u>small</u> and <u>easy to carry</u>. The most popular ones are the <u>pipe and tabor</u> (a three-holed recorder and a drum, played together for a one-man band effect), the <u>fiddle</u>, the <u>hurdy-gurdy</u>, the <u>bagpipes</u>, the <u>accordion</u> and the <u>concertina</u>.

These are the Main Types of Folk Music...

WORKSONGS
- British worksongs were made up by people like <u>farm workers</u>, <u>builders</u>, <u>sailors</u> and <u>miners</u>.
- They sang to take their minds off the grind of <u>hard labour</u>, and to help them work as a <u>team</u>.
- The songs are <u>unaccompanied</u> — the workers didn't have spare hands for playing instruments.
- Lots of songs were in <u>call and response</u> style. The '<u>shantyman</u>' sang the story and the other men joined in the <u>chorus</u>.

BALLADS
- Ballads tell <u>stories</u>.
- Some stories are made up — they tell stories from legends or about love affairs.
- Other ballads are about real events like shipwrecks or battles. Before <u>radios</u> and <u>television</u> when many people <u>couldn't read</u>, ballads were a way of passing on the news.

SHORT SONGS
- There are tons of shorter songs with <u>romantic</u> or <u>comic</u> lyrics.

DANCE MUSIC
- At events like <u>weddings</u> and <u>parties</u> people danced to <u>live music</u>.
- Lots of these dances are still around today — you still see people doing <u>Morris dances</u>, <u>sword dances</u>, <u>Scottish Highland dancing</u> and <u>Irish dancing</u>.

Folk Tunes are Fairly Simple

Some use <u>modal</u> scales. See P.15.

T'ain't simple. I'm usin' two 'ands.

1) A lot of folk <u>melodies</u> are based on <u>pentatonic</u> scales. They've only got <u>five notes</u>, which makes writing tunes with them lots easier.

2) A <u>major pentatonic</u> scale uses notes <u>1</u>, <u>2</u>, <u>3</u>, <u>5</u> and <u>6</u> of an ordinary <u>major scale</u>.

3) A <u>minor pentatonic</u> scale uses notes <u>1</u>, <u>3</u>, <u>4</u>, <u>5</u> and <u>7</u> of a <u>natural minor scale</u>.

4) There are <u>no semitone intervals</u> in pentatonic scales. It makes it much easier to add a <u>harmony</u> because the notes don't clash. It also makes them <u>easy to sing</u>.

The <u>structure</u> in folk tunes tends to be pretty simple too. They use forms like <u>binary</u> and <u>ternary</u> which have lots of repetition. <u>Songs</u> are often <u>strophic</u> — the tune stays the same for each verse. Phrases have even numbers of bars — usually <u>four</u>. Often each phrase begins with an <u>anacrusis</u> (see P.14).

And dosey-do...

Folk music is played by <u>ordinary people</u> — it's more beer and wellies than champagne and black tie. The main thing to remember is that the pentatonic scale makes writing melody and harmony <u>way easier</u>.

Baroque and Classical Melody

Baroque and classical music are similar but not the same. Here's a rough guide to both types...

Baroque Composers Used Major and Minor Scales

Baroque
1600–1750

1) From about 1600 Western composers stopped writing modal music (see P.15).
2) Instead they used major and minor keys to write tonal music. This was a big change. In Western countries like the UK most music is still tonal, hundreds of years later.
3) Modulating (switching between related keys, see P.30 in the Core book) turned out to be a good way of creating contrast in music.
4) Composers developed new structures for organising music using modulation and contrast, e.g. binary, ternary and rondo forms (see P.18).

Baroque has a Recognisable Sound

Baroque music's pretty easy to recognise. These are the main things to look out for in the Listening:
1) The dynamics change suddenly. Each bit is either loud or soft. You won't hear any gradual changes in volume — no crescendos or diminuendos. This is called terraced or stepped dynamics.
2) The melody's built up from short musical ideas (posh name = motives), so you get a fair bit of repetition.
3) The harmonies are simple. They mainly use chords I and V (chords covered on P.23 in the Core book).
4) The melody's swarming with ornaments added in to make it more interesting. (See P.21.)
5) The texture's often contrapuntal (polyphonic — see p31 of the Core Book).

The Harpsichord was Popular in Baroque Times

Baroque composers just loved harpsichords. If you hear a harpsichord in the Listening test, you can be 99.999% sure you're listening to a Baroque melody. Harpsichords were used as a solo instrument or to play the continuo part with an orchestra, filling in important harmonies.

Other Baroque instruments to listen out for are the flute, recorder, oboe, bassoon, organ and orchestral strings.

See Section 7 in the Core Content book for more on the instruments.

Baroque turned into Classical Music

Classical music grew out of baroque, so it's similar but not the same.
1) Classical tunes are very balanced. They tend to have equal four-bar phrases, split into a two-bar question and a two-bar answer.
2) Classical music uses fewer ornaments.
3) Classical composers still wrote in binary, ternary, rondo and variation forms, but they also came up with a new structure called sonata form (covered on P.38 in the Core book).
4) The dynamics are more subtle, using crescendos and diminuendos, not just changing suddenly.

Classical
1750–1820

New Instruments and Groups Changed the Sound

1) The piano was invented in about 1700. It got to be way more popular than the harpsichord because you could vary the dynamics. Classical composers went wild for the piano.
2) The clarinet was invented around this time too.
3) Orchestras got bigger — woodwind, trumpets and horns were used more and the string sections expanded.

Baroque and ba-roll was invented later...

In the Listening they could ask you who wrote the piece you're listening to. If you're stuck, try one of these:
Baroque — Bach, Handel, Vivaldi or Purcell, Classical — Mozart, Haydn or Beethoven. It'll lower the odds.

Baroque and Classical Structure

On these two pages I've helpfully *(gosh, I'm so helpful)* stuck the structures most often used by baroque and classical composers to give their melodies a <u>shape</u>. *And I've ironed your shirt and pants.*

Music in Binary Form has Two Sections

1) <u>Binary</u> means something like '<u>in two parts</u>' — there are <u>two bits</u> to a tune in <u>binary form</u>.

2) Binary form's usually used for <u>baroque dances</u>, e.g. bourrée, menuet, gavotte, sarabande and gigue.

3) Each section is <u>repeated</u>. You play Section A twice, and then Section B twice — so you end up with <u>AABB</u>.

4) Section B <u>contrasts</u> with Section A — the two parts should sound <u>different</u>.

5) The contrast's often made by <u>modulating</u> to related keys. Pieces in a <u>minor</u> key usually modulate to the <u>relative major</u>, e.g. A minor to C major. Pieces in a <u>major</u> key usually modulate to the <u>dominant</u> key (V), e.g. C major to G major.

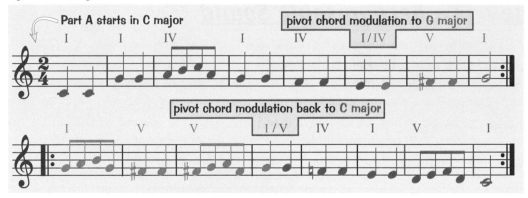

Ternary Form has Three Sections

1) <u>Ternary</u> means '<u>in three parts</u>' — there are <u>three sections</u> in music with ternary form. Each section <u>repeats</u>, so it goes AABBAA.

2) Section A ends in the <u>main key</u>, normally with a <u>perfect cadence</u> (see P.29 in the Core Content book). This makes it sound like a <u>complete piece</u> in itself.

3) In Section B the music modulates to a <u>related key</u>, like the dominant or relative minor, and then <u>goes back</u> to the main key before it ends.

4) When the music goes back to <u>A</u> for the <u>last section</u> it can be exactly the same <u>or</u> varied a bit. If it <u>is</u> varied you call it <u>A1</u> instead of A. A1 can be different, but not so different that you can't tell it's a variation of A.

> **MENUET & TRIO**
> * '<u>Menuet and trio</u>' is a ternary dance form from the Baroque and Classical periods.
> * <u>Section A</u> is the <u>menuet</u>, <u>Section B</u> is the <u>trio</u>. The menuet's repeated after Section B.
> * A menuet and trio is often used as the <u>third movement</u> of longer instrumental works such as <u>symphonies</u> and <u>sonatas</u>.

Rondo Form can have Any Number of Sections

1) <u>Rondo</u> means <u>going round</u>. A rondo starts with a main idea in <u>Section A</u>, moves into a <u>new section</u>, goes round again to <u>A</u>, moves into another <u>new section</u>, goes round again to <u>A</u>... as many times as you like. The <u>new section</u> after each Section A always <u>contrasts</u> with A.

2) Section A is known as the <u>main theme</u> or <u>refrain</u>. The contrasting sections are called <u>episodes</u>.

3) The main theme is always in the <u>main key</u>. Each <u>episode</u> tends to modulate to a <u>related key</u> for contrast.

Baroque and Classical Structure

Variations are pieces which start with one pattern or tune, and then change it in different ways.
There are two main structures for variation. In the Baroque and Classical periods composers loved
'em better than their own babies. They're called 'theme and variation' and 'ground bass'.

Theme and Variation Form Varies the Melody

1) In theme and variation form, the theme's usually a memorable tune.

2) The theme's played first. There's a short pause before the first variation's played, then another pause before the next variation. Each variation is a self-contained piece of music. There can be as many or as few variations as the composer wants.

3) Each variation should be a recognisable version of the main theme, but different from all the others.

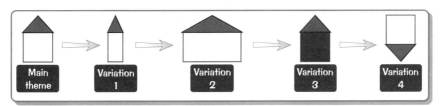

You can vary a tune in loads of simple ways:

Posh name = ornamentation

1) Start off with a basic theme...

2) Add notes to make the tune more complex.

3) Remove notes to simplify the tune.

4) Change the metre — say, from two beats in a bar to three.

5) Add a countermelody — an extra melody over the top of the theme.

6) You can also: change the tempo; change the key; change some or all of the chords; add a different type of accompaniment, e.g. a classical 'Alberti bass' pattern instead of block chords.

7) There are some more ways of varying melodies on P.20 and P.21.

Ground Bass Form Varies Ideas Over a Fixed Bass Part

Ground bass is a continuous set of variations — there are no pauses. The main theme — called the ground — is a bass line which repeats throughout the piece. Varying melodies and harmonies which become gradually more complex are played over the ground. There are two types of baroque dance that are in ground bass form — the chaconne and passacaglia. They're quite slow and stately.

Freshly ground bass — it goes all powdery...

None of these structures is horrifically complicated — but it's easy to get one muddled up with another. These are good pages to learn painstakingly, tediously thoroughly so you can be sure you know what's what.

Baroque and Classical Melody Patterns

These are some of the more <u>sophisticated</u> ways Baroque and Classical composers developed their melodies. Look out for them in your <u>Listening</u> exam, and try to use some in <u>your compositions</u>.

Melodic Inversion — *Turning the Tune Upside Down*

1) <u>Melodic inversion</u> makes a melody sound very different, but not totally different.

2) You keep the <u>same intervals</u> between the notes, but they go in the <u>opposite direction</u>, i.e. down instead of up, and up instead of down. Basically you turn the tune on its head.

The first melody goes <u>up a major third</u> from C to E, then up a minor third to G.

In the inversion the melody goes <u>down a major third</u> to A♭, then down a minor third from A♭ to F.

Retrograde — *Playing the Tune Backwards*

Playing the notes <u>in reverse order</u> is called <u>retrograde</u>.

If you switch the notes so they're in reverse order <u>and</u> inverted, you get a <u>retrograde inversion</u>.

Sequencing — *Repeat a Pattern, Vary the Pitch*

1) Repeat the <u>pattern</u> of a phrase but start on a <u>different note</u>, higher or lower. This is called a <u>sequence</u>.

2) <u>Rising</u> sequences go up in pitch. <u>Falling</u> sequences go down.

Imitation — *Repeat a Phrase with Slight Changes*

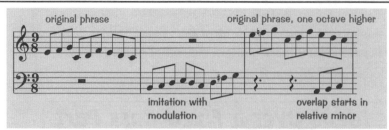

1) In <u>imitation</u> a phrase is repeated with <u>slight changes</u> each time.

   In imitation a phrase is repeated with slight changes each time.

2) It works particularly well if one instrument or voice imitates <u>another</u> and then <u>overlaps</u>.   *It works particularly well if one instrument or voice imitates another and then overlaps.*

Ostinato — *Keep One Pattern the Same, Change the Rest*

1) This is called ostinato. One pattern's played <u>over and over</u> again.

2) The rest of the piece <u>changes round it</u>.

Here's the repeating pattern

Baroque and Classical Melody Patterns

Another way of livening up a melody that was <u>VERY POPULAR</u> with baroque composers was adding in <u>ornaments</u>. Ornaments are fiddly <u>little notes</u> that stand out a bit from the main tune.

A Trill is Lots of Tiny Quick Notes

1) In baroque music the trill starts one note <u>above</u> the written note then goes quickly back and forth between the written note and the note you started on.

2) In classical music the trill starts <u>on</u> the written note and goes up to the note above.

3) The <u>second-last note</u> is usually the one <u>below</u> the written note.

4) A <u>sharp</u>, <u>flat</u> or <u>natural</u> sign above the trill symbol tells you if the note to trill to is sharp, flat or natural.

HERE'S HOW YOU PLAY A TRILL IN CLASSICAL MUSIC

The trill lasts the same length of time as the written note.

Appoggiaturas Clash with the Chord

1) An appoggiatura <u>clashes</u> with the accompanying chord.

2) The note <u>before</u> it is usually quite a <u>jump</u> away.

3) The note <u>after</u> the appoggiatura is always <u>just above</u> or <u>below</u>. It's called the <u>resolution</u>. The <u>resolution</u> has to be from the <u>accompanying chord</u>.

4) Appoggiaturas usually fall on a <u>strong beat</u>, so the resolution note falls on a <u>weaker beat</u>.

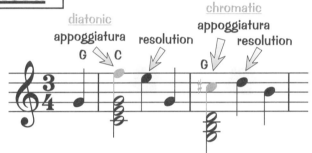

Passing Notes Link the Notes Before and After

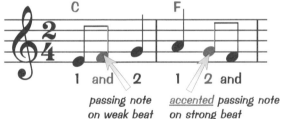

passing note on weak beat

<u>accented</u> passing note on strong beat

1) A passing note <u>links</u> the notes before and after it. The notes before and after have to belong to the <u>accompanying chord</u>.

2) They're usually put on <u>weak beats</u>. When they <u>are</u> on the strong beat they're called '<u>accented passing notes</u>'.

Turns are Set Patterns of Notes

A turn starts on the note <u>above</u> the written note, then goes to the <u>written note</u>, followed by the note <u>below</u> the written note. It ends back on the <u>written note</u>.

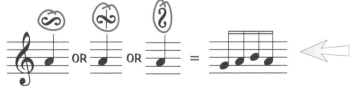

An <u>inverted turn</u> starts on the note <u>below</u> the written note, then goes through the written note, then the note above that, and finally back to the written note.

I've done my bit — now it's your turn...

All the stuff in this section about Baroque and Classical tells you how they put the <u>melody line</u> together. If you want to find out more about writing <u>harmonies</u>, have a squizz at Section 4 in the Core Content book.

The 20ᵗʰ Century — Atonality

In the <u>early 20ᵗʰ century</u> composers started seriously monkeying around with the way melodies were written. They <u>dumped</u> Classical-style <u>tonal</u> music. No major and minor scales for 20ᵗʰ century composers. No siree.

Romantic Composers Started the Move Away from Tonality

The big changes to Art music in the twentieth century didn't just appear on the concert hall stage in a puff of green smoke. They developed from changes that were <u>already happening</u> during the Romantic period.

> The <u>Romantic</u> period runs roughly from <u>1820 to 1900</u> — it fills the gap between Classical music and the twentieth century. <u>Schumann</u>, <u>Chopin</u>, <u>Verdi</u> and <u>Puccini</u> are some of the famous Romantic composers.

1) Classical music is <u>tonal</u> — the key a melody's written in gives it a definite <u>character</u>.

2) Romantic composers used a lot of <u>chromatic</u> notes — notes that didn't belong to the main key of a melody.

3) The Romantics bunged in so many chromatics that their music started to <u>lose</u> the character of the main key.

4) By the twentieth century a lot of music sounded like it didn't belong to any key at all. Music that doesn't sound like it comes from any particular key is called <u>atonal</u>.

More chromatics... I must have more chromatics...

The change from <u>tonal to atonal</u> music doesn't sound that dramatic on paper, but it was a really <u>big change</u>. The old forms like binary, ternary and rondo (P.18) <u>didn't work</u> any more because they relied on fixed keys to create <u>contrast</u> between the different sections. Composers had to come up with whole new ways to <u>structure</u> their music.

Debussy Wrote Melodies with a Whole Tone Scale

Debussy was a French composer — he started writing music in the Romantic period and carried on till <u>1918</u>, so he saw a lot of changes. Debussy's big innovation was to compose using a <u>whole tone scale</u>. He didn't invent whole tone scales, but he wasn't shy about using them. If you start a whole tone scale on C, this is what you get...

In the whole tone scale <u>all</u> the notes are a tone apart. None of them stands out in a melody, and you don't get that character from the piece being in a certain key that you do with major and minor scales — so a melody written using a whole tone scale is <u>atonal</u>.

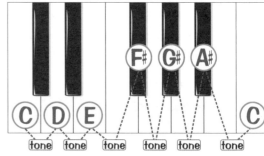

1) The whole tone scale makes melodies sound <u>hazy</u> and <u>dreamy</u>.

2) Debussy's style is sometimes described as <u>impressionist</u> — the same word used to describe the '<u>out of focus</u>', blurred effect of work by <u>painters</u> like Monet and Manet.

3) Debussy added to the impressionist effect with <u>colourful chords</u> (with added <u>9ths</u> and <u>13ths</u>) and by picking instruments with exactly the right <u>timbre</u> to play different melodies.

So Romantic... So Dreamy... Aaah...

When you do the Listening test, and you're writing about posh classical music from the 20ᵗʰ century, it's safest to call it <u>twentieth century art music</u>. It makes it clear you don't mean the <u>Classical period</u>.

The 20ᵗʰ Century — Serialism

You don't have to like Schoenberg's style of music (I don't), but you <u>do</u> have to learn about it...

Schoenberg Invented a 12-note System called Serialism

Schoenberg was a composer born in Vienna, in Austria, in 1874. In the early part of his life he composed in a style reasonably similar to other <u>Romantic</u> composers who were around at the time — but his music moved from <u>highly chromatic tonality</u> to <u>atonality</u>.

In the 1920s he came up with a completely <u>new way</u> of structuring atonal music. It's called the <u>12-note system</u> (because it uses twelve notes) or <u>Serialism</u> (because the notes are used in a series).

12 Notes are Arranged and Rearranged

To compose a serialist piece, Schoenberg would start by arranging the <u>12 chromatic notes</u> of an octave in a set order. This starting point was called the <u>Prime Order</u>:

The notes of the Prime Order were <u>rearranged</u> to create a piece of music.

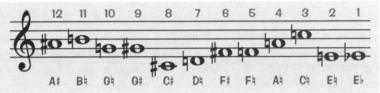

PRIME ORDER IN RETROGRADE
Notes in reverse order

PRIME ORDER INVERTED
Intervals between notes turned upside down

PRIME ORDER IN RETROGRADE INVERSION
Inverted notes in reverse order

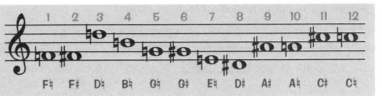

PRIME ORDER TRANSPOSED
Notes of prime order (or one of the variations) shifted up or down — these are moved 2 semitones

Remember — Schoenberg DIDN'T just play notes at random...

Serialism wasn't just Schoenberg's baby — he had two students called Berg and Webern who composed in Serialist style too. But Schoenberg's the one to blame... *oops, um... er... slip of the tongue...* I mean <u>praise</u> for coming up with Serialism in the first place. Listen, learn and enjoy.

The 20th Century — Serialism & Microtonal

Here's how Schoenberg turned his <u>tone rows</u> into an actual piece of music...

The Snippets of Melody Combine as a Complete Piece

Once Schoenberg had all his variations on the Prime Order, he could use these patterns of notes as <u>building blocks</u> to create a complete piece of music.

1) Notes from the prime order, or any of the variations, could be played in the <u>bass line</u> or <u>melody</u>, and in <u>any octave</u>.

2) Groups of notes from the prime order and variations could be piled up to make <u>chords</u>. Notes that were next door to each other in the original rows would be played all at once by different instruments. This is called <u>verticalisation</u> — notes that were written out horizontally in the rows would be written out <u>vertically</u> in the score.

3) The prime order could be designed to create decent-sounding chords with <u>triads</u>.

4) The prime order could also be designed to create <u>cluster chords</u> with notes really close together.

cluster chord

FAC triad

Because serialist music is built up from short sections, it tends not to have long sweeps of melody like you hear in other styles of music. Instead it sounds a bit like little <u>snippets</u> of sound, played at <u>random</u>. It's sometimes described as <u>pointillist</u> after a style of painting that uses hundreds and thousands of tiny dots to create an image, instead of long brushstrokes.

Microtonal Music is Even Weirder than Serialism

1) In <u>traditional</u> music the smallest gap between notes is normally a <u>semitone</u>. In <u>microtonal</u> music there can be much smaller gaps between notes — it's all up to the composer what the exact tuning of the notes is.

2) A microtonal scale could use <u>quarter tones</u>, so you'd have 24 notes in an octave. Or, a composer could split the octave up in a completely different way, e.g. with <u>unevenly spaced</u> notes, or notes that are all very <u>close together</u>.

3) Microtonal music can sound quite <u>weird</u> if you're not used to it, because the smaller gaps between notes don't sound like 'proper' intervals. It can sound out of tune, or it can just sound a bit boring because there's less movement between notes.

4) Microtonal music is often played on <u>synthesisers</u>. The gaps between notes aren't 'standard', so a synthesiser is useful because you can program in the <u>exact tuning</u> for each note of the scale.

Microtonal music — it's a tiny bit different...

It's no good me going on, trying to describe serialism or microtonal music in words — this really is something you have to <u>hear for yourself</u>. Have a look on the internet for downloadable files you can listen to. You're not going to find this stuff in Woolies, that's for sure.

The 20ᵗʰ Century — The Blues

Blues is another style of music that gets a lot of its flavour from the scales it uses.

African Slaves in America Started off the Blues

Blues is a combination of African and European musical styles. It first started
on the slave plantations of the southern United States in the nineteenth century.

1) In the 1600s and 1700s hundreds of thousands of Africans were captured and sold as slaves.
   They were taken to work on plantations in North America.

2) To pass the time and take their minds off the work, which was often brutally hard,
   they sang worksongs, using their tools to give the music a beat.
   The lyrics were often about the hardship and misery of living as a slave.

3) Over the years, African musical styles like call and response singing blended with features
   of European music, especially chords. This combination was the beginning of the blues.

4) Even after slavery was finally abolished in the 1860s, ex-slaves living in the southern states
   were poor and powerless. The lyrics and tone of their songs carried on being sad and 'blue'.

5) The traditional blues instruments are harmonica, guitar, banjo, violin, piano, double bass and
   the voice. They're all acoustic — electric instruments hadn't been invented when blues began.

6) In the early twentieth century black Americans started playing the blues in bars and clubs
   beyond the southern states. By the 1920s blues was massively popular all over America with
   white and black audiences.

Blues has its Own Scale

1) You get a blues scale by flattening
   the third and seventh of any major scale
   by a semitone. The fifth note's sometimes
   flattened too.

2) The flattened notes are known as the
   blue notes.

3) The blue notes are notes that were 'bent'
   in African singing. The singers would
   'slide' up or down to a note, giving it a
   twang and making it slightly flatter.

4) The second and sixth notes are often left out.

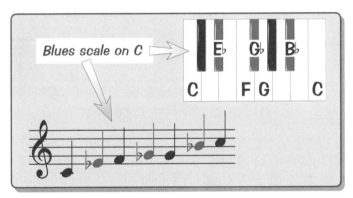

Blues Melodies have Swinging Offbeat Rhythms

1) In normal 'straight' rhythm the
   beats split up into equal halves.

2) In the blues, the first bit of the beat nicks some time from
   the second bit. The first bit ends up longer and with more
   oomph. This gives the music a swinging feel.

3) The blues uses lots of syncopation (see P.45 in the Core
   Content book). You get a lively offbeat sound by avoiding
   the strong beats — it puts the oomph in unexpected places.

   (ahem)

The 20th Century — The Blues

There are lots of different types of blues, but the most popular song structure is the 12-bar blues.
Ladies and gentlemen — let's hear a big hand for... the 12-bar blues...

12-bar Blues Repeats a Twelve-Bar Structure

12-bar blues is a set chord pattern, twelve bars long. Singers like Bessie Smith
and Robert Johnson made the 12-bar blues structure really popular in the 1920s
— it's been around ever since and is still one of the most popular styles.

BAR 1	BAR 2	BAR 3	BAR 4
Chord I	Chord I	Chord I	Chord I

BAR 5	BAR 6	BAR 7	BAR 8
Chord IV	Chord IV	Chord I	Chord I

BAR 9	BAR 10	BAR 11	BAR 12
Chord V	Chord IV	Chord I	Chord I

To lead back into bar 1
you play chord V in bar 12
instead of chord I.

1) The only chords are I, IV and V.
   (See P.23 of the Core Content book.)

2) The twelve-bar pattern's repeated right through the song.

3) You can make the chords even more bluesy by adding the
   minor 7ths (see P.22 in the Core Content book).

> 12-bar blues has had a huge influence on other musical styles
> including ragtime, jazz, rock and roll and R&B. Loads of pop
> songs today still use the standard 12-bar structure.

Twelve Bars Breaks Nicely into Three Lines

The twelve-bar chord pattern of 12-bar blues breaks up nicely into three lines, each with four bars.
The lyrics of a 12-bar blues song usually stick to three lines for each verse of the song.

Lines 1 and 2 are usually the same.

Line 3 is different, but
rhymes with lines 1 and 2.

> *Woke up this morning feeling blue.*
> *Woke up this morning feeling blue.*
> *Feeling sad and lonesome without you.*

The words are usually pretty gloomy.

Each line takes up 4 bars, but the words don't always fill up the whole line.
The singer's bit — the call — is followed by an instrument playing an
answer — the response — in the gap before the next line.

You can have any colour you like so long as it's blue...

The blues doesn't have to be mournful, sad and depressing — it just sounds better that way... If you
fancy writing a blues piece for the Terminal Task remember to use all the things that make the blues
sound like the blues — blue notes, swinging rhythm, three-line verses and call and response.

Indian Classical Music

The examiners call this bit 'Indian Classical Music'. The music's great, but you need to make sure you can spell all the words if you want to write about them in the exam.

Indian Classical Music is based on Ragas

1) A raga is a set of notes (usually between 5 and 8) which are combined to create a particular mood.

2) Ragas use a scale similar to the western 12-note scale, but it is not tempered. This means that there is not an equal distance between consecutive notes. In fact, the pitch of one note can vary within a single raga.

3) Many ragas are always performed at a particular time of day, or during a particular season.

4) In Northern India, raga students join a school of players called a gharana. Each gharana is run by a teacher or master, and each gharana has its own traditions and theories about how to play.

5) Spirituality is an important part of almost all Indian Classical Music. In Southern India, there is a long tradition of the Karnatic kriti. This is a raga set to words in praise of a particular Hindu deity.

The Traditional Instruments are Sitar, Tambura and Tabla

SITAR

1) A sitar is a large, long-necked string instrument.

2) Sitars have between four and seven main metal strings. On a seven-string sitar, five are plucked for the melody and the other two create drone notes.

3) Sitars also have 'sympathetic' strings underneath the main strings. The sympathetic strings vibrate when the main strings are played, creating a thick, shimmery sound.

4) The frets on a sitar can be moved — they're adjusted to different positions for different pieces.

5) Sitar players can pull strings to make notes 'bend' or distort.

6) Sliding a finger along a string as it's plucked gives a sliding glissando sound called mind.

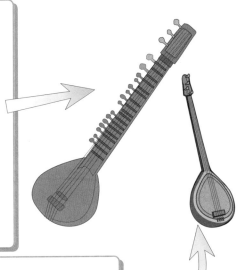

TAMBURA
The tambura's a similar shape to the sitar but has just four metal strings. It's used as more of a backing instrument.

TABLA
Tabla is a pair of drums. The smaller, right-hand drum is called tabla. The larger, lower-sounding drum is called the baya.

OTHER INSTRUMENTS ARE USED TOO...

1) The sarod — a mini-sitar with a fretless fingerboard.
2) The sarangi — a small, bowed stringed instrument with no frets.
3) The bansuri — a flute made of bamboo.
4) The shenhai — an instrument with a double reed, like an oboe.
5) The harmonium — a keyboard instrument powered with air pumped by foot-pedals.
6) Singers sometimes perform with the instruments too.

Can we have a tabla for four, please...

Some people find it tricky to get to grips with Indian Classical Music because it's so different from the music they're used to. That's precisely why the examiners make you study it — you're supposed to be amazed at the great and glorious diversity of music.

Indian Classical Music

Each instrument in raga has a different job. The <u>sitar</u> plays the <u>melody</u>. The <u>tabla</u> play the <u>rhythm</u>.
You'll have to wait till the next page to find out about the tambura. Can you bear the <u>suspense</u>...

The Melody is Improvised on the Sitar

1) In a classical Indian group the sitar plays the <u>melody</u>.

2) The sitar player <u>improvises</u> the melody. He or she chooses a scale called a *raga*
    (just like the style of music), and makes up the melody using notes from that scale.

3) There are <u>hundreds</u> of different *raga* scales. Each one is named after a different <u>time of day</u> or <u>season</u>.
    Each raga's supposed to create an <u>atmosphere</u> like the time or season it's named after.

4) Each raga scale is a set of <u>ascending</u> and <u>descending</u> notes.
    The notes on the way up can be different from the ones on the way down.

5) Some ragas have rules for individual notes in the scale. There could be notes that are always played <u>quickly</u>,
    notes that have to be <u>decorated</u>, or notes have to be played <u>tivra</u> (slightly sharp) or <u>komal</u> (slightly flat).

6) The notes of a *raga* scale are called
    <u>sa</u>, <u>ri</u>, <u>ga</u>, <u>ma</u>, <u>pa</u>, <u>dha</u> and <u>ni</u>.
    Unlike Western scales, *ragas* don't
    always have the full set of notes.

RAGA VIBHASA — DAWN RAGA

SA RI GA MA DHA NI DHA MA GA RI SA

7) Sometimes the melody part's taken
    by a <u>singer</u> instead of the sitar.

The Tabla is the Rhythm Section

1) The main rhythm is played on the <u>tabla</u>.

2) The tabla player plays a rhythm called a <u>tala</u> with a set number of beats (called <u>matras</u>).
    There are hundreds of talas, just like there are hundreds of ragas.

3) The <u>first beat</u> of a tala is called the <u>sam</u>. <u>All</u> the performers in a group
    <u>play together</u> on each sam and the whole piece always <u>ends</u> on a sam.

4) Each tala is split into groups called <u>vibhags</u>. A vibhag is a bit like a <u>bar</u> in Western
    music, except that you can have different numbers of beats in each vibhag.

5) One, or sometimes two, vibhags in a tala have a <u>different sound</u> from the others — this section's
    called the <u>vibhag khali</u>. For contrast, the vibhag khali is played on the <u>smaller</u> tabla drum.

6) As well as playing the tala, tabla players improvise <u>more complicated rhythms</u>
    over the top. They can vary their sound with different <u>finger positions</u>, and
    by <u>speaking</u> the beat (with syllables like <u>dhin</u> or <u>ta</u>) as they play.

7) Sometimes the <u>audience</u> joins in, and claps along with the tala. They clap at the beginning of each vibhag.
    In the vibhag khali they do a quiet clap, called a <u>wave</u>, tapping the back of the right hand into the left.

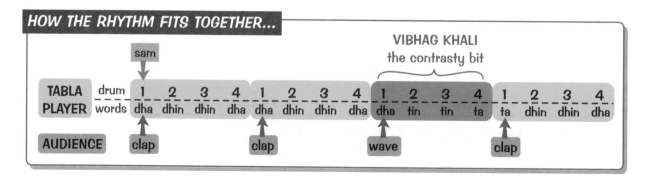

Indian Classical Music

To complete the sound of *raga* you add the <u>tambura</u> to the sitar and tabla.

The Tambura Creates the Harmony

1) The <u>tambura</u>'s job in a raga performance is to create the <u>harmony</u>. The sitar part's a bit like the right-hand part in a piano piece and the tambura's like the left.

2) The tambura's part is often described as a <u>drone</u>. It's not quite as boring as the name suggests, but it is quite <u>repetitive</u>. The tambura player plays a <u>simple rhythmic pattern</u> based on just <u>two notes</u> from the *raga* all the way through the performance.

3) The sitar player works his or her improvisations <u>around</u> the tambura part — and it's the combination of the two that gives the raga harmony.

Usually the drone uses the '<u>sa</u>' and '<u>pa</u>' notes, but the one for the Raga Vibhasa uses '<u>sa</u>' and '<u>dha</u>'.

SA DHA DHA SA

I'll do the droning round here if you don't mind.

A Typical Raga has Four Sections

The tradition is for a raga performance to have <u>four phases</u>.
There are <u>no gaps</u> between the different phases — each one flows into the next.

1 THE ALAP

The <u>sitar</u> player introduces the notes of the chosen <u>raga scale</u>, improvising freely. There's <u>no beat</u> or pulse to the melody at this point — it just flows along. The only accompaniment at this point is the <u>tambura drone</u>.

2 THE JHOR

In this second section, the music <u>speeds up</u> a bit. It's still just the tambura player and sitar player, but the music gets more rhythmic, and the melody improvised by the sitar player takes on a <u>steady beat</u>.

3 THE JHALA

This section is <u>loads faster</u> than the alap and jhor, and feels a lot more exciting than the bits that came before.

4 THE GAT OR BANDISH

In the gat, the *raga* really takes off.

• The <u>tabla player</u> comes in — at last.

• The group plays a <u>pre-composed</u> piece. It's called 'gat' if it's for instruments only, and 'bandish' if there's a song.

• The players also add improvisations to the gat or bandish, and pass their musical ideas around in a sort of musical <u>question and answer</u>.

Make sure you know your vibhag from your vibhag khali...

I reckon the trickiest bit here isn't <u>understanding</u> it — it's remembering the massive number of words that are completely new unless you've studied Indian Classical music before. But they're just words — like <u>egg</u> and <u>car park</u>. Close the book and scribble down all those technical words and what they mean. And keep at it.

Revision Summary

When people say Jupiter, or an elephant, or K2, or the Great Wall of China is big, they don't know what they're talking about. They don't know the meaning of big. They haven't seen this section. They haven't seen the groaning mass of facts that's been levered in with a giant crowbar.
They haven't felt the weight of all those facts pressing down on their fragile little skulls. You have. I have. We know the meaning of big. That was one monster of a section. To top it off and check you've really got the facts licked, here's a monster of a Revision Summary...

1) Write down a definition of 'melody'.

2) Explain what each of these words means when you're talking about melody:
   a) contour   b) range   c) phrasing   d) structure   e) anacrusis.

3) What group of people sang a lot of plainchant? Where did they sing it?

4) What's unusual about the rhythm of plainchant?

5) What's antiphony?

6) Write down the note names of the Phrygian mode beginning on E.

7) Why do most modes sound different from major and minor scales?

8) Name six instruments used for playing folk music.

9) What type of scales are most folk tunes based on? Why?

10) When did the Baroque period start and end?

11) What did Baroque and Classical composers use instead of modes?

12) Are you more likely to hear a harpsichord in a Baroque composition or a Classical composition?

13) What type of harmonies did Baroque composers often use?

14) When did the Classical period start and end?

15) Write down as many differences as you can between Baroque and Classical music.

16) What structure is this describing?
    The first section's in G major. There's a modulation and the next section's in D major. After this section you hear section one again. The fourth section's in E minor. The last section's a repeat of section one.

17) Explain how you use each of these to vary a melody:
    a) augmentation   b) diminution   c) melodic inversion   d) retrograde
    e) retrograde inversion   f) sequence   g) imitation

18) Starting on the G above middle C, write out: a) a trill   b) a turn.

19) Write out a whole tone scale starting on D.

20) What style of painting is compared to whole tone music?

21) Who invented serialism?

22) In serial music, what's the Prime Order?

23) What's verticalisation?

24) Why is serial music described as pointillist?

25) Write a three-sentence history of the blues.

26) Write out a blues scale starting on G.

27) What's the difference between straight and swinging rhythm?

28) Write two verses of blues lyrics in the standard three-line format.

29) What's a tala?

30) Which instrument in Indian classical music plays the drone?

31) Describe the sections of a typical raga performance.

32) From the whole of Section 3, write down five types of scale that melodies can be based on.

33) Right, that's it, see ya.

Dance Music — The Basics

Metre, tempo, rhythm and phrasing are the absolute basics in dance — they're the bits
in the music that tell the dancers when and how to move. Here's how they work...

The Pattern of Beats is Called the Metre

The beats in a piece of music make
different patterns of strong and
weak beats, depending on the time
signature. The pattern they make is
called the metre.

Nearly all dance music has a regular
metre. The strong beats make the
same pattern throughout the music.

> **THE MAIN METRES USED IN DANCE ARE...**
>
> *DUPLE METRE*
> 2 beats per bar. It goes 'TUM tum, TUM tum'.
>
> *TRIPLE METRE*
> 3 beats per bar. It goes 'TUM tum tum, TUM tum tum'.
>
> *QUADRUPLE METRE*
> 4 beats per bar. It goes 'TUM tum TUM tum, TUM tum TUM tum'.

The Tempo tells Dancers How Fast to Move

1) The movements in a dance normally fit the speed of the beat — the tempo.

2) The speed of a dance does a lot to set the mood.
A pavan has a controlled tempo matching the stately movements, but
a carefree Irish jig, with a lot of leaping about, has a zippier tempo.

3) Dance music that's written for listening to is often written with lots of
speeding up and slowing down.

4) In dance music that's actually used for dancing the tempo stays the same all
the way through a piece to make it easier for the dancers to follow the beat.

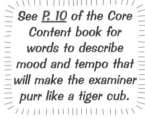

*See P. 10 of the Core
Content book for
words to describe
mood and tempo that
will make the examiner
purr like a tiger cub.*

Dance Moves Often Follow the Rhythm

Some dances have a set rhythm that goes with
set movements. E.g. in tango, the 'arm out,
strut across the floor and throw your partner back'
move fits a repeated rhythm in the music.

In formal dances the set movements often match regular phrases in the music. The phrases
are usually 4 bars long. When a new phrase begins the set movements are repeated.

There are Different Types of Dance

Dads at weddings dance by jiggling from foot to foot, but there are loads of other types of dance:

1) CEREMONIAL DANCE — in some cultures there are traditional dances for important occasions,
e.g. at Greek weddings there are special dances which all the guests join in with.

2) COURT DANCE — for celebrating official occasions like coronations or royal weddings.

3) SOCIAL DANCE — dances which take place in ballrooms/parish halls/discos/clubs.

4) FOLK DANCE — Morris dancing, maypole dancing and other dances performed at public events.

5) DANCES THAT TELL STORIES — like in classical ballet.

6) INSTRUMENTAL DANCE MUSIC — music that's written in the style of a dance, but meant for listening, not
for actual dancing, e.g. some of the waltzes, polkas and menuets written by Chopin, Brahms and Schubert.

Show the examiners you know all the moves...

Dance is one of the Areas of Study they test in the Listening. That means you need to know all the jargon
for talking about dance. You need to know it so well that it trips off your tongue quicker than a flock of
ballerinas in pink satin ballet shoes, all wearing tutus, with their hair scraped into amazingly tight buns.

Pavan and Galliard

Pavan and galliard is the type of dance you see in films like *Elizabeth*, *Romeo and Juliet* and *Shakespeare in Love*. The pavan part is slow and formal, with plenty of time for flirting with your dancing partner.

Pavan and Galliard is a Court Dance

1) Queen Elizabeth I ruled England from 1558 to 1603.
2) Elizabeth was a cultured old bird and encouraged lots of different art forms. She sponsored writers like Shakespeare and she wasn't a bad poet herself.
3) Elizabeth was into music, too. The royal household was full of music and dance.
4) Pavan and galliard was one of the most popular dances at Elizabeth's court. It was danced by several couples at a time at big, formal parties.
5) The most popular pavan and galliard composers were John Bull, William Byrd, Thomas Morley, Orlando Gibbons and Giles Farnaby.

John Bull was astonished to discover that he was not a fictional character.

The Pavan Contrasts with the Galliard

The pavan and galliard are quite different styles of dance, but they were usually played as a pair — first the pavan and then the galliard.

THE PAVAN

1) The pavan's in duple metre — that's two beats per bar.
2) It's played at a slow tempo and the dance steps are performed at a steady, even walking pace.
3) The movements are grand and stately like in a procession for an important official occasion.
4) This rhythm's often repeated in the accompaniment of a pavan: ♩ ♩♩ | ♩ ♩♩ |

THE GALLIARD

1) The galliard is written in triple metre — three beats per bar.
2) The galliard has a fast tempo and the dance steps — high jumps and kicks in the air — match the liveliness of the music. Lots of dotted and syncopated rhythms give a jumpy offbeat feel.

To make the pavan and galliard go together as a pair, composers used similar melodic ideas in both.

The Structure Uses a lot of Repetition

1) Pavan and galliard has a pretty simple structure using lots of repetition and variation.

> Section A — the opening section, usually eight bars long
> Section A1 — a repeat of A with some variation
> Section B — a new section
> Section B1 — a repeat of Section B with some variation
> Section C — new section
> Section C1 — a repeat of Section C with (you guessed it) some variation

2) To create the variation composers liked to use a technique called divisions.

The longer notes are divided into shorter notes.
The new short notes move up and down in patterns like scales.

3) The last chord of pavans and galliards was often repeated several times — meanwhile the couples took turns bowing to each other to end the dance.

Pavan and Galliard

So much for the structure. How did they actually play this pavliard-gallivan-thingy...

The Band was Called a Consort

1) The music for pavan and galliard, and other posh court dances, was played by a group called a consort.

2) A consort's more like a band than an orchestra because there's just one of each instrument.

3) A band made up of instruments of the same type (e.g. different sized recorders) was called a whole consort. A band with instruments from different families was called a broken consort.

4) The type and size of consort depended on the number of people coming to the dance — lots of people meant you needed a bigger, noisier band so the music could be heard.

These Instruments Were Used to Play Pavan and Galliard

LUTE & THEORBO

A lute is an instrument similar to a guitar. It's a stringed instrument with frets that you play by plucking. The big difference from a guitar, apart from the shape, is that the strings were tuned in pairs, called 'courses'.

The theorbo is basically a really big lute that was used to play the bass line for dances. It's sometimes called the chitarrone.

RECORDER

Elizabethan recorders had whistle-mouthpieces and were made of wood. There were as many as eight different sizes — sopranino, two different sopranos, alto, tenor, bass, quint bass and great bass.

VIOL

Viols look a bit like violins, but they're played upright (not under the chin), they have six strings, and the fingerboard has frets. Viols come in three sizes — treble, tenor and bass.

CRUMHORN

The crumhorn's a wooden wind instrument, curved at the end like a walking stick. It has a double reed, like an oboe. The four sizes are soprano, alto, tenor and bass.

PIPE AND TABOR

The pipe and the tabor are two instruments played as a pair. The pipe looks a bit like a recorder, but only has three holes so you can play it with one hand. The tabor's a small drum that you hang round your neck and play with the other hand.

VIRGINALS

Pavan and galliard was sometimes written for the virginals — an early keyboard instrument. Virginals are fairly quiet so they weren't used for actual dancing, just playing a tune.

Twentieth Century Composers Wrote Pavans Too

Pavans made a comeback in the twentieth century — Ravel, Vaughan Williams and Warlock all wrote pavans. They mixed the older style of music, which gave their compositions a feeling of looking back in time, with new ideas about melody and harmony.

Do you know your crumhorn from your theorbo...

Whenever I think of recorders, I can almost taste the saliva-plus-disinfectant mixture the ones in our primary school had. Well, banish all thoughts of squeaky primary school recorder groups — when it's played properly, the recorder has a wonderfully rich, mellow sound.

Viennese Waltz

No marks will be awarded for ballgowns, coiffure, sequins or rictus-grin.
However, <u>marks will be awarded</u> for your knowledge of musical aspects of the Viennese waltz.

The Waltz Craze Started in Vienna

1) People first started writing and dancing waltzes in <u>Austria</u> — mostly in the ballrooms of the capital, <u>Vienna</u>.
2) The first waltzes were written in the <u>1790s</u>.
3) The waltz ended up being one of the most popular dances of the nineteenth century — not just in Vienna, but all over <u>Europe</u> and in <u>North America</u> too.
4) People thought the waltz was really <u>saucy</u> at first — it was the first dance ever where people held each other so <u>closely</u>.

The Rhythm Goes 'Oom Cha Cha, Oom Cha Cha'

1) A waltz is always in <u>triple metre</u>. The time signature's usually <u>3/4</u>.
2) Viennese waltzes go pretty <u>fast</u> — about 70 bars a minute (a bit faster than a bar a second).
3) The '<u>oom</u>' is <u>stronger</u> than the 'cha cha', so the rhythm <u>feels</u> more like <u>one beat in a bar</u> than three.
4) The 'oom cha cha' rhythm is emphasised in the <u>accompanying chords</u>.

OOM cha cha   OOM cha cha   OOM cha cha   OOM cha cha

In performance the second beat of each bar is played <u>slightly early</u>. Pulling the beat about like this is called <u>rubato</u> — the effect in a waltz is to make it sound even more lively.

The Chords are Simple and Don't Change Much

A waltz has a <u>strong clear tune</u>, closely backed by the chords. It's called a <u>homophonic texture</u> — see P.31 in the Core book for more on texture.

1) The chords are pretty simple — mostly they're the <u>primary chords</u> I, IV and V.
2) The same chord's used for <u>at least one bar</u>, and sometimes two or four bars.
3) <u>One note</u> of the chord's played on the 'oom'. On the 'cha cha' the <u>rest of the notes</u> are played together, or the whole chord's played.
4) The speed of chord changes is called the <u>harmonic rhythm</u>. Waltz chords change slowly, so waltzes have <u>slow</u> harmonic rhythm.
5) This slow, simple chord pattern can get a bit repetitive, so composers use <u>appoggiaturas</u> (P.21) and <u>chromatic notes</u> to spice up their tunes.

Here's a bit of a waltz by <u>Johann Strauss the Younger</u> ()

*Tying notes over the bar adds a touch of <u>syncopation</u>.
The accents in bar 3 add syncopation too.*

*This is a <u>chromatic appoggiatura</u> —
A♯ doesn't belong in the key.*

This is the <u>first note</u> of a <u>C chord</u>.

These are the rest of the notes in the <u>C chord</u>.

This in an <u>inverted G7 chord</u> with the <u>3rd in the bass</u>.

<u>Viennese Waltz</u>

And-a <u>one</u>, <u>two</u>, <u>three</u>, one, two, three, one, two, three, one...

<u>Waltzes Started Simple and Ended Up Complex</u>

The first waltzes were written in <u>binary</u> <u>form</u> with two 8-bar repeated sections.

SECTION A	SECTION A repeated	SECTION B	SECTION B repeated

waltz 1	SECTION A	SECTION A repeated	SECTION B	SECTION B repeated
waltz 2	SECTION A₁	SECTION A₁ repeated	SECTION B₁	SECTION B₁ repeated
waltz 1	SECTION A	SECTION A repeated	SECTION B	SECTION B repeated

Pairs of waltzes were grouped together to make <u>ternary form</u> pieces.

Two Viennese composers — <u>Joseph Lanner</u> and <u>Johann Strauss the Elder</u> added various bits and bobs to make waltzes <u>longer</u> and more <u>complex</u>. A later waltz has...

1) *A SLOW INTRODUCTION*   In the introduction you hear stuff like wavering strings (posh word = <u>tremolo</u>), <u>arpeggios</u> (probably on the harp) and little <u>tasters</u> of the main tunes on the woodwind instruments.

2) *FIVE OR MORE WALTZ TUNES*   Each waltz includes several different tunes, all in <u>related keys</u>. Each tune lasts between <u>16</u> and <u>32 bars</u> and is in <u>binary</u> or <u>ternary</u> form.

3) *A CODA*   This is a <u>final section</u> that rounds off the waltz by pulling together bits from all the tunes.

> *There were lots of waltzing Strausses:*
> *The dad was <u>Johann Strauss the Elder</u>, and he had three sons*
> *who all composed waltzes — <u>Johann</u>, <u>Josef</u> and <u>Eduard</u>.*
> *Johann Strauss the Younger composed two of these longer-style*
> *waltzes — <u>Tales from the Vienna Woods</u> and <u>The Blue Danube</u>.*
> *Each one lasts about <u>ten minutes</u>.*

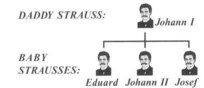

DADDY STRAUSS: *Johann I*

BABY STRAUSSES:
Eduard Johann II Josef

...Apparently they all looked quite similar too. Although it's <u>just possible</u> I made that up so I didn't have to find pictures of all of them ;-)

<u>Viennese Waltzes were Played by Big Orchestras</u>

Viennese waltzes were played by the <u>large orchestras</u> that were standard in the <u>Romantic period</u>.

There's a lot of <u>brass</u> and <u>woodwind</u>, including more unusual instruments like piccolos.

The percussion sections have a big <u>variety</u> of instruments, e.g. timpani, tambourine, triangle and snare drum.

<u>Waltzes Spread Beyond the Ballrooms</u>

Waltzes got to be so popular during the nineteenth century that they spread into other types of music.

1) Waltzes crop up as <u>dances</u> and <u>songs</u> in <u>operettas</u>. Some of the more famous ones are by <u>Johann Strauss the Younger</u> (e.g. *Die Fledermaus*) and <u>Gilbert and Sullivan</u> (e.g. *Pirates of Penzance*).

2) Waltzes were so popular in the nineteenth century that people liked to play them at home on the piano. <u>Chopin</u>, <u>Schumann</u>, <u>Brahms</u> and <u>Weber</u> all wrote tons of waltzes for playing at home, as well as harder virtuoso waltzes for concert pianists.

3) Some nineteenth century composers included waltzes in their <u>orchestral works</u>, e.g. Berlioz's *Symphonie Fantastique*, Tchaikovsky's *4th* and *5th Symphony*, and Ravel's *La Valse*.

4) Tchaikovsky put waltzes in his <u>ballets</u> too — *Swan Lake* and *Sleeping Beauty* both include waltz tunes.

5) In the twentieth century the waltz was used in a few <u>musicals</u>. There are waltzes in Cole Porter's *High Society* and Rogers and Hammerstein's *The Sound of Music*.

<u>The Viennetta waltz is similar, but more chocolatey...</u>

A waltz ought to be pretty easy to spot in the Listening — basically if you can say '<u>oom cha cha</u>' in time to the music, it's more than likely to be a waltz. *(But try to say it quietly, or people will think you're playing trains.)*

Disco Music

Disco is cheesy. Disco is in bad taste. Disco is shameless. The dancing was embarrassing. The clothes were awful. The make-up was unspeakable. Still, I gotta admit... it gets <u>everyone</u> on the dancefloor.

Disco was the Dance Music of the 1970s

Before disco

DISCO

Disco first reared its groovy head in nightclubs in the <u>USA</u>. The roots of disco were in <u>soul</u>, <u>jazz</u> and <u>funk</u>. Disco was played in clubs and it <u>totally changed them</u>...

1) Until about the 1960s <u>audio equipment</u> was pretty ropey — you couldn't play a recording loud enough to dance to, so most clubs had live bands.

2) In the 1970s, <u>amplifiers</u>, <u>turntables</u> and <u>loudspeakers</u> got loads better. Suddenly you could play records loud enough to fill a club with sound. **DJs** took over from band leaders as the important people in a club.

3) People danced <u>on their own</u> rather than in pairs and they really enjoyed <u>showing off</u> their groovy dance moves and flashy outfits.

4) <u>Lighting technology</u> got more exciting too — <u>flashing lights</u> and **effects** became part and parcel of the experience of a night out in a club.

The Strong Beat and Catchy Tunes Made Disco Easy to Like

1) Disco tunes are almost always in <u>4/4</u>. They're played at around <u>120 beats per minute</u>.

2) The simple beat makes disco tunes really <u>easy to dance to</u> because just about any dance move will fit. People loved this because it gave them the freedom to make up their <u>own moves</u>.

3) People also liked the <u>catchy tunes</u>. Every disco tune has a <u>hook</u> — a short stab of <u>tune</u>, a <u>word</u> or a <u>phrase</u> that sticks in people's minds so they remember (and buy) the record.

Aah aah aah aah Stayin' alaaiii... aiii... aii... ive.. WOO...

Disco Songs have a Verse-Chorus Structure

A disco tune will almost always start with an <u>intro</u>.

* The introduction does two jobs — it grabs people's <u>attention</u> and <u>sets the mood</u>.
* Intros often use the best bit from the rest of the song to make people <u>sit up and listen</u>.

After the intro, the structure of a disco song basically goes <u>verse-chorus-verse-chorus</u>...

* All the verses usually have the <u>same tune</u>, but the <u>lyrics change</u> for each one.
* The chorus has a <u>different tune</u> from the verses, usually quite a catchy one. The lyrics and tune of the chorus <u>don't change</u>.
* In a lot of songs the verse and chorus are both <u>8 bars long</u>.

One verse, or the middle 8, can be switched for an <u>instrumental section</u>.

The old verse-chorus thing can get repetitive. To avoid this most songs have a <u>middle 8</u>, or bridge, that sounds different. It's an <u>8-bar section</u> in the <u>middle</u> of the song with <u>new chords</u>, <u>new lyrics</u> and a whole <u>new feel</u>.

The song ends with a <u>coda</u> or <u>outro</u> that's <u>different</u> to the verse and the chorus. In disco it usually <u>fades out gradually</u> so the DJ can <u>mix</u> the end of one song with the beginning of another.

Disco Music

One of your coursework compositions can be a disco tune. No, seriously, it can. To get that full-blown disco sound you need to use a good mixture of <u>acoustic</u> and <u>electric</u> instruments. These are the main ones...

Electric Guitars Play Lead and Rhythm Parts

The guitar sound in disco is pretty distinctive.

1) As with most pop music up to the 1980s the <u>main instruments</u> in a disco line-up are the <u>electric guitars</u>.
2) The <u>lead guitar</u> plays the <u>solo tunes</u>.
3) The <u>rhythm guitar</u> strums <u>chords</u> along with the beat.
4) The strings on the rhythm guitar are often <u>muted</u> by pressing down with the side of the hand. This stops the chords from ringing on and makes them sound more <u>percussive</u>.

An electric guitar has six strings tuned to E, A, D, G, B and E. It has to be plugged into an amplifier and loudspeaker.

Bass Guitars Play Short Riffs

Most disco music has <u>short</u>, <u>rhythmic</u>, <u>heavy-sounding</u> bass riffs.

The bass guitar works in the same way as the electric guitar, except it has four strings, tuned to E, A, D and G. Bass guitarists pick out the individual notes of a bass line — they don't play chords.

Brass and Strings Beef Up the Sound

1) <u>Sweeping string sounds</u> give the music a real meaty sound by filling the gaps between the other sounds.
2) Brass instruments are used to add in an occasional '<u>parp parp</u>'. They're called <u>stabs</u> and they almost always fall on an <u>offbeat</u>.

Disco uses Drum Kits, Drum Machines and Sequencers

You hear acoustic <u>and</u> electronic drum kits playing alongside each other on many disco tracks.

1) The low <u>bass drum</u> plays every crotchet beat.
2) The <u>snare drum</u> mostly plays on beats <u>2</u> and <u>4</u>. The <u>hi-hat</u> plays <u>offbeat quavers</u>.
3) This basic drum rhythm plays <u>all the way through</u> the song.

The little circle means the hi-hat's played open — so it rings on.

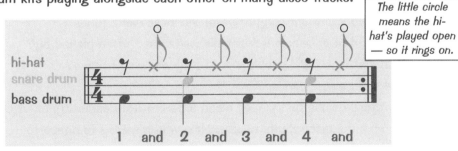

Extra percussive sounds like <u>hand claps</u> are often added by <u>drum machines</u>. Disco also creates backing <u>loops</u> using <u>sequencers</u>. Short snippets of music, e.g. bass lines, tunes, chords and rhythms, are recorded on sequencers. They're <u>played repeatedly</u> through the recording. Loops are usually made so they'll <u>fit together</u> in different combinations.

Don't blame it on the sunshine — blame it on examiners...

Listen to the Beegees soundtrack from the film <u>Saturday Night Fever</u>. Better still, if you haven't seen it already, watch the film — you'll get a first-hand feel for the groovy fashions and dance moves of the disco era. If you want to hear more disco try <u>The Jackson Five</u>, <u>Earth, Wind and Fire</u> and <u>Donna Summer</u>.

Revision Summary

Look at these beautiful freshly picked revision questions. They may not look like much at first glance, but every one's a corker. The true inner beauty of these little gems is that you can use them to check you know everything you need to know from this section. So get testing yourself, and remember, you only <u>really know</u> your stuff when you can answer all the questions without looking back through the book. That's the difference between <u>knowing</u> and <u>looking up</u>.

1) Write a definition of metre (in music, not maths).
2) What effect does the tempo of a piece of music have on the dancers?
3) Why don't you get lots of tempo changes in dance music?
4) Why are the phrase patterns in dance music regular?
5) Name five different types of dance.
6) What events was pavan and galliard played at?
7) Name three composers who wrote pavan and galliard.
8) Describe the metre, tempo and dance movements in a pavan.
9) Describe the metre, tempo and dance movements in a galliard.
10) How did composers link the two parts of pavan and galliard?
11) What are 'divisions' in pavan and galliard?
12) What's the difference between a whole consort and a broken consort?
13) Why didn't people dance to pavan and galliard that was played on the virginals?
14) Write a short description of each of these Elizabethan instruments:
    a) lute   b) theorbo   c) crumhorn   d) recorder   e) pipe and tabor   f) viol
15) Name two twentieth century composers who have written pavans.
16) Where did the waltz start its rise to fame?
17) In what years was the waltz most popular?
18) Describe the rhythm of a waltz.
19) What does tempo rubato mean?
20) The texture of a Viennese waltz is homophonic. What does 'homophonic' mean?
21) How would you describe the harmonic rhythm of a waltz?
22) Name three ways composers introduced variety into waltzes.
23) What was the structure of a typical early waltz?
24) Describe the structure of later waltzes.
25) Name two important composers of Viennese waltz tunes.
26) What kind of ensemble is Viennese waltz most often played by?
27) What instrument did people use to play waltzes at home?
28) Where did disco start up?
29) What made clubs that played disco different from earlier types of club?
30) Describe the disco rhythm and explain why it's easy to dance to.
31) What's a hook?
32) What's the usual structure for a disco song?
33) What's the difference between the lead guitar part and the rhythm guitar part in disco music?
34) What acoustic instruments would you expect to hear on a disco track?
35) Write out a standard percussion line for a disco track.

Fusion

I'd like to say a brief word about jam. I was planning to put lots of jam sandwiches on this page, but according to our printers, jam plays havoc with their machinery. So you'll just have to make do with fusion.

Fusion is Combining Musical Styles

This section's about three musical styles called salsa, bhangra and minimalism. All three began when musicians from one tradition took on ideas from other traditions. Creating new styles like this is called fusion.

Musicians are always borrowing ideas from other traditions to liven up their music.
They take the ideas and mix them in with their own style.

Sometimes two styles fuse when someone just thinks, "I wonder what it would sound like if I added in X..." and hits on a great new sound which becomes popular with other musicians.

More often styles fuse when two cultures are thrown together. The slave trade from Africa to North America brought Africans into contact with the Europeans who had moved over there. Over time African and European styles mixed and new styles like blues appeared. *(See P.25 and P.26 for more on blues.)*

> *Salsa, bhangra* and *minimalism* are all fairly recent. For a bit of background the rest of this page covers ways composers have combined styles in the past.

Composers Borrowed Musical Ideas from Other Countries

Composers have often found great new ideas in music from other countries.
1) Mozart and Haydn used the bass drum and cymbals in their symphonies.
   At the time this was a new idea — the bass drum and cymbals came from Turkey.
2) Debussy, Ravel and Britten all used sounds from Indonesian gamelan music.

Some Classical Composers Borrowed from Folk Music

1) Up until the nineteenth century composers pretty much ignored folk music. They were mostly paid by aristocrats and royalty who would have thought folk music was a bit common.
2) In the nineteenth and twentieth centuries attitudes and society in Europe changed. Revolutions like the French Revolution (1789) and the Russian Revolution (1917) took power away from the aristocracy and made working class people and their culture more important.
3) Composers started to be more interested in the folk music played by ordinary people, and to include it in their work. They borrowed features like melodic intervals and dance rhythms common in their national folk tunes, and combined them with classical traditions. They also used whole tunes as themes for overtures and symphonies.
4) Some of the more famous composers who've used use folk music are:

> *CHOPIN* (1810–1849) based many pieces on Polish national dances, e.g. the polka and mazurka.
>
> *SMETANA* (1824–1884) used elements of Czech folk music and folk tales in his music, e.g. 'Ma Vlast' (which means 'My Country') and the opera 'The Bartered Bride'.
>
> *BELA BARTOK* (1881–1945) travelled round Hungary recording folk music, partly so the old tunes wouldn't be forgotten, and partly looking for ideas to use in his own work.
>
> *AARON COPLAND* (1900–1990) used cowboy tunes from the United States in his piece 'Rodeo'.

Musical fission is when one style splits into two...

Do you want to hear some good news? Do you really? I'll tell you then. You won't get directly tested on the stuff on this page. Phew. But you do need to understand what fusion is and understand that it's something that's always been going on in music. So no learning here, just make darn sure you understand.

Salsa

Salsa is a tasty dip for tortilla chips. It's also a lively type of <u>Latin American dance music</u> which blends the <u>son style</u> from Cuba with elements of <u>jazz</u>. The next few pages are about <u>musical</u> salsa.

Salsa Grew out of Son

The <u>Spanish</u> colonised Cuba and brought <u>African slaves</u> to work there on the sugar plantations. Over the years, music from the two cultures <u>combined</u> to make a dance style called <u>son</u>. Son is the <u>main ingredient</u> of salsa. Traditional son music has:

1) A basic repeated rhythm pattern called a <u>clave</u> (pronounced *CLAH-VEY*) played by hitting two sticks called <u>claves</u> (pronounced *CLAYVES*) together.

2) <u>More</u> repeated rhythm patterns played on percussion instruments like the <u>maracas</u> and <u>bongos</u>. These parts are often <u>syncopated</u> and form complicated <u>cross-rhythms</u> against the clave part.

3) <u>Call and response</u> (p36, Core book) between the lead singer (called the <u>sonero</u>) and the chorus (the <u>choro</u>).

4) Mainly <u>primary chords</u> (I, IV and V) in the harmony.

5) Harmonies in <u>3rds</u> and <u>6ths</u>.

6) The <u>last note</u> of a bar in the <u>bass line</u> often sets up the harmony for the <u>following bar</u>.

The Clave is the Key to any Son Tune

The clave is the <u>basic rhythm</u> of a piece of son music. It's the bit you <u>tap your feet to</u>. The son clave rhythm has a group of <u>three</u> notes and a group of <u>two</u>.

It goes like this...   ...or like this...

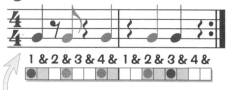

This one's called a <u>3-2 son clave</u>.   This one's called a <u>2-3 son clave</u>.

Have a go at <u>clapping</u> out the rhythm. <u>Count out loud</u> as you clap to make sure you're getting it right. Don't be surprised if you find it fairly <u>tricky</u> at first.

A piece of son music uses the same clave all the way through. All the other parts <u>fit round it</u>. This bit from the chorus of a song called 'The Peanut Vendor' uses a <u>2-3 clave</u>.

The clave rhythm <u>isn't played</u> in every single son tune — but you can still <u>feel it</u> in the rhythm of other parts like the bass line.

There's a Special Clave for Rumba

There are different clave rhythm patterns to go with <u>different dances</u>. The clave for a <u>rumba</u> goes like this:

The <u>rumba clave</u> has a group of three and a group of two notes, just like the son clave — but the <u>last note</u> of the group of three is <u>delayed</u> by one quaver. It's a small difference, but has a big effect.

I thought this happy lady was dancing rumba. But she wasn't. Oh well.

Salsa

Son's the basic <u>Cuban</u> ingredient of salsa. In 1930s <u>New York</u>, son was mixed with big-band jazz. This was the beginning of salsa, which is now massively popular all over Latin America.

Big-Band Jazz Combined with Son to Make Salsa

In the <u>1930s</u>, thousands of Cubans and Puerto Ricans migrated to <u>New York</u>. Musicians took bits of the <u>American big-band jazz style</u> and combined it with <u>son</u> — the result was salsa.

Salsa is basically son, with these features of big-band thrown in:

- *SYNCOPATION* — a lively offbeat rhythm
- *JAZZ CHORDS* — 7ths, 9ths and other chords with added or altered notes
- *RIFFS* — short repeated phrases
- *IMITATION* — one section of the band repeats a part just played by another section, e.g. the woodwind section might imitate a bit the brass section's just played
- *WALKING BASS LINES* — bass parts that move in crotchets, playing the notes of the chord with the odd passing note to fill the gaps
- *COMPING* — playing rhythmic chords on piano or guitar to accompany the tune.

The Salsa Band Combines Son and Big-Band Instruments

A traditional son band's called a <u>sexteto</u>. It has six instruments: <u>guitar</u>, <u>string bass</u>, <u>bongos</u>, <u>maracas</u>, <u>claves</u> and the <u>tres</u>, which is a bit like a guitar but with three sets of two strings.

As the salsa style developed and picked up <u>influences from big-band</u>, more instruments were added. These are the main sections in a <u>modern salsa band</u>:

FRONT LINE or HORNS

There are usually one or two <u>trumpets</u> or <u>saxophones</u> which play the tune.

VOCALS

There are one or two <u>soneros</u> (lead vocalists) and the <u>choro</u> (the chorus).

RHYTHM SECTION

This could have <u>piano</u>, <u>guitar</u>, <u>bass</u>, traditional Latin American percussion instruments like <u>congas</u>, <u>timbales</u>, <u>bongos</u>, <u>maracas</u>, the <u>guiro</u>, and sometimes a standard <u>drum kit</u>.

BONGOS (and other drummish things)
Bongos are paired drums played with the hands.
Congas and timbales are also paired drums.
(Congas look similar to bongos, but taller. They're also played with the hands. Timbales look quite a bit different from bongos and congas — they're made from metal and plastic rather than wood and skin. Timbales are played with metal sticks.)

GUIRO
makes a scrapy noise

MARACAS

You say clave — I say clave...

One of the most famous people to mix up son and big-band was the trumpet player <u>Dizzie Gillespie</u>. He was American. But salsa's <u>Latin American</u>. And a clave is a completely different thing from a <u>clave</u>. And a horn is a <u>saxophone</u> or <u>trumpet</u>, not a French horn. And I'm not confused and you're not confused. Not at all.

Salsa

Half a billion Latin Americans can't be wrong — salsa is gorgeous, fantastic and back for a <u>third page</u>.

A Salsa Tune has Three Main Sections

There are <u>three main chunks</u> in a salsa tune. The three different chunks can appear in <u>any order</u>, and they can all be used <u>more than once</u>.

1) In the <u>verse</u> you hear the main tune, usually sung by the <u>sonero</u> or played by an instrumentalist.

2) The <u>montuno</u> is a kind of chorus where the sonero or lead instrumentalist improvises and the choro or other instrumentalists answer.

3) You'll also hear a break between choruses, called the <u>mambo</u>, with new musical material, e.g. different chords or a different tune. It's often played by the horn section. They either <u>layer</u> their parts to create a <u>harmony</u>, or <u>stagger</u> the parts, so one group plays and is quickly followed by another and another...

4) You're also likely to hear an <u>introduction</u> and <u>ending</u>.

5) There could also be a 'break' — a bit where the main tune <u>butts out</u> and just the rhythm section plays.

Here's a fairly <u>typical</u> salsa structure:

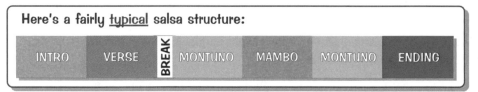

| INTRO | VERSE | BREAK | MONTUNO | MAMBO | MONTUNO | ENDING |

The <u>timbale</u> player plays a <u>drum roll</u> called an <u>abanico</u> at the <u>start</u> of each new section. Listen out for it — it'll help you work out when the sections are <u>changing</u>.

The Rhythms Change in Each Section

Happy, oh so happy, in my happy salsa dance.

The <u>conga</u>, <u>bongo</u> and <u>timbale</u> parts all change between a verse and montuno or mambo.

1) The <u>conga</u> player uses <u>two drums</u> in the <u>montuno</u> and <u>mambo</u>, but just <u>one</u> in the <u>verse</u>.

2) The <u>bongo</u> player switches to a <u>cowbell</u> and a different <u>rhythm</u> in the montuno and mambo.

3) The <u>timbale</u> player plays the <u>mambo bell</u> as well as the timbale in the <u>montuno</u> and <u>mambo</u>.

Have a look at these percussion parts. Take it <u>one line at a time</u> or it could get confusing...

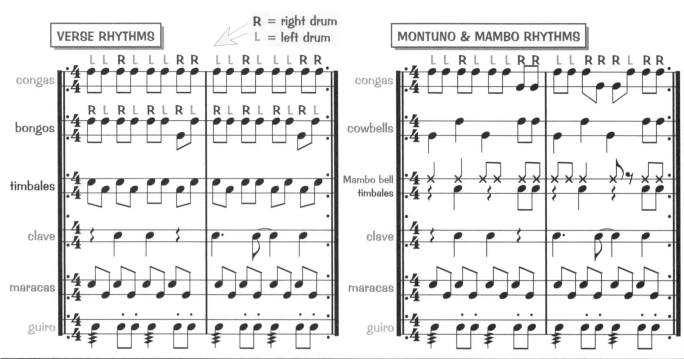

If you were Cuban you'd have to learn all this in Spanish...

It's no good just reading about salsa. You've got to <u>listen to it</u>, <u>have a go at playing it</u> and <u>try writing some</u> so you can get your head round all those tricky clave rhythms. Better still, get your teacher to arrange a class <u>field trip to Cuba</u>. I'm sure it's completely practical and quite cheap really. And the beaches are great.

Section Five — AoS4: Traditions and Innovation

Bhangra

Bhangra mixes <u>traditional</u> dance rhythms and tunes from <u>India</u> and <u>Pakistan</u> with <u>club-style dance music</u>. Bhangra tunes have a <u>narrow range</u>. It's quite common for the <u>widest</u> interval to be a <u>minor 3rd</u>. This means that tunes often only use a <u>few repeated notes</u>.

Bhangra was Originally a Folk Dance

1) Traditional bhangra's a type of <u>folk music</u> from the <u>Punjab</u> — an area in northern India and Pakistan.
2) It's played at <u>harvest time</u> when people dance and sing to celebrate the end of the harvest.
3) The key instrument is the <u>dhol</u>, a <u>double-headed</u>, <u>barrel-shaped</u> <u>drum</u>. Each drum head has a different sound. One is much <u>lower</u> than the other.
4) These are two of the <u>traditional rhythms</u> in bhangra:

CHAAL	The most popular rhythm for traditional and modern bhangra is the <u>chaal</u>.

1) It's an <u>eight note</u> repeated pattern.
2) The quavers are <u>swung</u> like in the blues (see P.25).

DHA NA NA NA NA DHA DHA NA

BHANGRA RHYTHM	This rhythm is used in some bhangra too, but it's not as popular as the chaal.

DHA NA NA GE GE NA DHA NA NA GE GE NA

The words that go with the beats are called <u>bols</u>. They help players remember the <u>drum strokes</u> for the rhythm...

NA = play the <u>small</u> drum head.
GE = play the <u>large</u> drum head.
DHA = play <u>both</u> drum heads.

Modern Bhangra Developed in the UK

1) The modern bhangra style developed in the <u>UK</u> in the <u>1980s</u>.
2) Asian musicians fused the chaal rhythm with western styles like <u>hip-hop</u>, <u>disco</u>, <u>drum and bass</u>, <u>rap</u> and <u>reggae</u>, making bhangra much more popular with mainstream audiences.
3) They also used western instruments like <u>bass guitar</u>, <u>electric guitar</u> and <u>synthesizers</u>.
4) Bhangra's still really popular with young Asians in the <u>UK</u> and <u>abroad</u>.

> The band <u>Alaap</u> took bhangra to audiences outside the Asian community with the hit song <u>Bhabiye Ni Bhabiye</u> in the 1980s. Other well-known bhangra performers are <u>Malkit Singh</u>, <u>Sahotas</u> and <u>Panjabi MC</u>.

Modern Bhangra Uses Lots of Music Technology

<u>Music technology</u> plays a big part in modern bhangra. Listen out for...

1) <u>Remixes</u> — tracks with lots of different <u>layers</u> mixed together in <u>new ways</u>. A remix normally sounds very different from a live performance because so much has been changed in the studio.
2) <u>Samples</u> from other music, e.g. <u>bass lines</u>, <u>drum parts</u>, <u>words</u> or <u>other sounds</u> mixed in with the new track.
3) <u>Drum machines</u> instead of the dhol.
4) DJ techniques like <u>scratching</u>.

Some people dance to bhangra — YOU have to learn it...

You probably don't remember the 1980s all that well — you probably weren't even <u>born</u>. Well, I've got a major confession to make. <u>I</u> remember the 1980s. I remember how everyone went on about bhangra as the next <u>big thing</u>. What's worse I wore some truly horrible clothes and there are <u>photos</u> to prove it.

Minimalism

Minimalist painting is painting with just a few lines or squares. Minimalist <u>music</u> is music that just changes a <u>tiny weeny subtle bit</u> at a time. Some people might call it boring, but don't say that to an examiner.

Minimalism Builds Music out of Loops

1) Minimalism's a <u>western art music</u> style that developed during the <u>1960s</u> and <u>1970s</u>.
2) It's made up of constantly repeated patterns called <u>loops</u>. The loops are <u>short</u> and <u>simple</u>, but the final music can get quite <u>complicated</u> — especially the <u>rhythm</u>.
3) There's <u>no real tune</u> — you can't sing along to minimalist music.
4) The <u>harmonies</u> are made by <u>layering patterns</u> one on top of the other. They take a <u>long time</u> to <u>change</u>.
5) Some of the 'big names' in minimalism are <u>Steve Reich</u>, <u>Philip Glass</u> and <u>Terry Riley</u>.

When you first start listening to minimalist music it sounds like it hardly changes at all, but as you get used to it and '<u>tune in</u>' you'll start to notice the tiny changes to the repeated loops. People often describe minimalist music as having a '<u>hypnotic</u>' quality — it kind of hypnotises you.

These are the Main Techniques for Changing the Loops

These different ways of changing the loop patterns are used in most minimalist pieces:

NOTES ARE GRADUALLY ADDED OR TAKEN AWAY

One note is <u>added</u> on each repetition of the pattern — this is called <u>additive melody</u>.

Another similar idea is to <u>replace one note with a rest</u>, or one rest with a note on each repetition.

THE NOTES OF THE PATTERN CHANGE OVER TIME

This technique's called <u>metamorphosis</u> — an unnecessarily long word for 'changing'. Tiny changes to <u>one note</u>, or <u>one bit of the rhythm</u>, are made in each repetition.

Often the changes go <u>full circle</u>, so the pattern ends up the <u>same</u> or nearly the same as it was at the start.

ADDING OR REMOVING NOTES OR RESTS

Two or more performers start with the <u>same pattern</u>. On each repeat, a note or rest is <u>added</u> or <u>taken away</u> from one of the parts. This changes the <u>length</u> of the pattern in the different parts.

They move gradually <u>out of sync</u> and then gradually back in. The proper name for this is <u>phase shifting</u>.

LAYERING DIFFERENT LENGTH PATTERNS TOGETHER

This one's called '<u>layering</u>'. You play loops of <u>different lengths</u>, e.g. a 4-beat loop and a 5-beat loop, <u>at the same time</u>. You get a similar effect to phase-shifting — the patterns move <u>apart</u> then come back <u>together</u>.

Minimalism

Have you seen a film called _The Piano_... This woman gets her finger chopped off with an axe, ends up having an affair with Harvey Keitel, who has all-over body tattoos, and nearly drowns. And it has a minimalist soundtrack.

Music Technology Plays a Big Part in Minimalism

Minimalism has always used a lot of electronic bits and bobs to put music together.
When composers first started writing minimalist music in the 1960s, they had a bit of a challenge
on their hands, because music technology was a lot less sophisticated than it is today...

1) The repeated loops were played using old-fashioned tape recorders —
   the ones you see in old spy films with two massive wheels for the tape.

2) Composers made loops by carefully cutting a tape so it just had the bits of
   music they wanted, then sticking the cut ends together.

3) The loop was played by running it out of the tape player and around something
   smooth, like a bottle or mike stand, so it could keep going round and round.

4) They didn't just use loops of music. They made loop recordings of words and
   other noises too — it's a bit like modern sampling.

5) The different loops were put together using multitrack recording. They were
   recorded, one on top of another, to create the layered sound of minimalism.

6) Even live performances of minimalist music often make use of recorded
   backing tracks, played alongside the live instruments.

Steve Reich and _Terry Riley_ are two of the minimalist composers who came up with this technique for looping._

Minimalism Uses Musical Ideas from All Over the World

Minimalists didn't just sit around in libraries waiting for inspiration to strike.
Most of them have borrowed ideas from other countries and other cultures.

West African music is based mainly on the rhythm. The master drummer leads changes in the patterns.

West African music uses complex cross-rhythms.

Gamelan (from Indonesia) has layered parts, all playing versions of the same tune, but at different times.

POLYRHYTHM

RHYTHM MORE IMPORTANT THAN TUNE

LAYERING

MINIMALIST MUSIC

HARMONIES CHANGE SLOWLY

Gamelan doesn't use harmony at all.

LOOPING

PIECES LONG AND HYPNOTIC

Most non-Western music's based on looping, e.g. the tala rhythm in raga (see P.28) is a constant loop.

Some Indian and gamelan pieces go on for days.

The drone in raga plays the same harmony all the way through.

Tune, tone, lone, line, lint, lent, bent, belt, bell, bull, dull...

Minimalism can take a bit of getting used to, because the tune just isn't that important.
It's those tiny continual changes to the rhythm and texture that you're supposed to listen out for.
On the plus side though — at least minimalist music's going to be dead easy to recognise in the listening...

Revision Summary

Not so fast, my little chickadee. Just because that was the last section of the book doesn't mean you can go skipping my delumptious Revision Summary questions. Use the section to help you answer the questions to start with, but you should be able to answer <u>all</u> the questions <u>without</u> looking <u>before</u> you close this book. Got it... Good... Then let us begin...

1)   What do you call it when styles from two different musical traditions combine?

2)   Which two traditions are combined in blues and jazz?

3)   Name one composer who used ideas from Turkish music and one who used ideas from Indonesian music, <u>before</u> the twentieth century.

4)   Why did composers basically ignore folk music before the nineteenth century?

5)   Name three things that composers borrowed from folk music and used in their work.

6)   Name a composer who went out and collected folk tunes.

7)   List six main features of the Cuban son style.

8)   Write out the son clave, either on a stave or with a box diagram.

9)   What's the difference between a 3-2 son clave and a 2-3 son clave?

10) Write out the rumba clave.

11) What North American musical tradition combined with son to make salsa?

12) Name a famous jazz musician who was interested in Latin American music.

13) List the jazz ingredients of salsa. *(You should be able to think of at least six.)*

14) Which instruments are you likely to hear in the front line of a salsa band?

15) Which instruments are you likely to hear in the rhythm section of a salsa band?

16) What are the three sections of a piece in salsa style called?

17) What happens in each of the three sections of a salsa piece?

18) Write out salsa percussion rhythms for:
     a) bongos   b) timbales   c) maracas   d) congas

19) Where is traditional bhangra played?

20) When would you expect to hear traditional bhangra?

21) What's the name of the traditional drum that plays the chaal?

22) Write out the chaal rhythm.

23) Explain what each of these bols means:
     a) dha   b) na   c) ge

24) Where and when did modern bhangra develop?

25) List as many Western styles as you can that have been mixed with traditional bhangra.

26) Write down four ways music technology is used in modern bhangra.

27) What's the name of the bhangra band that had the first major bhangra hit in the UK?

28) When did minimalism develop?

29) What are loops?

30) Describe:
     a) additive melody   b) metamorphosis   c) phase shifting   d) layering

31) Describe how a tape loop works.

32) Explain what each of the following musical traditions has in common with minimalism:
     a) Indian classical music   b) West African music   c) Indonesian gamelan music

Air Guitar

Air guitar is a relatively new musical style. It developed about 20 or so years ago, when Mr Osbourne was famous for biting bats' heads off rather than moaning about his wife's dogs on Sky TV.

Air Guitar uses the Same Techniques as Real Guitar

First things first. Playing air guitar is exactly the same as playing a real guitar. The only difference is there's no guitar. So, like any beginner (real) guitarist, you need to learn some basic techniques:

1) Learn how to hold your 'guitar'. Find one that matches your size, and practise holding it in the right position. Always practise this in front of a mirror.

2) Get the stance right. Your feet should be at least 60 cm apart*.
For general posture ideas, think caveman/woman.
   * *This is only true if you're playing rock music from the 70s onwards. For example, if you were playing 50s-style rock'n'roll you would need an entirely different stance — feet together, no movement from waist down, top half of body swaying from left to right, cheesy grin...*

3) Make sure you always look like you're concentrating *really really* hard.
This is particularly important during widdly bits.

60 cm

4) Hair time. If you don't have long hair, it's very important that you pretend you do have long hair. Move the head forwards and backwards in time with the music, throwing your hair everywhere. If you're doing it properly you should soon notice your hair starting to stick to your sweaty face and get caught in your mouth and nose. Perfect this hair technique and you're well on your way.

You need to Learn the Three Classic Moves:

The 'Down-on-One-Knee' Manoeuvre is Easy

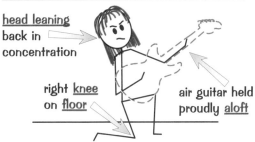

head leaning back in concentration

right knee on floor

air guitar held proudly aloft

'The Windmill' Takes a Bit More Practice...

right hand forming perfect circles

The trick is getting the circle to pass through the point where you would hit the strings (if you were playing a real guitar). This requires both technique and confidence. It's easy to look like a nonce if you mess it up.

...and you need Spandex Pants to do the 'Star Jump'

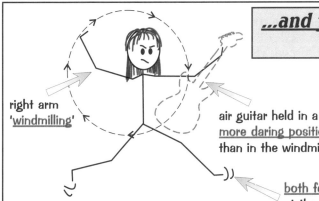

right arm 'windmilling'

air guitar held in a more daring position than in the windmill

both feet kicking outwards at the same time

WARNING:
The star jump should only be attempted by the professional air guitarist. Appropriate clothing must be worn — spandex pants really are the only way to go.

Air guitar — don't knock it till you've tried it...

And finally... I'd like to finish off the page with a list of recommended tunes to practise air guitar to.
1. Sweet Child of Mine (G'n'R)   2. Eye of the Tiger (Survivor)   3. Bohemian Rhapsody (Queen)
4. Run to the Hills (Iron Maiden)   5. Livin' on a Prayer (Bon Jovi)   6. Money for Nothing (Dire Straits)

Glossary and Index

As I'm sure you're all-too-painfully aware, there's a staggering number of technical terms that you're expected to learn for GCSE Music. So I thought a bit of a glossary-type-thing wouldn't go amiss here...

12-bar blues Style of blues with a 12-bar repeating chord pattern. **26**

12-note system The system created by **Schoenberg** in the 1920s, which involves rearranging the 12 chromatic notes of an octave into a set order. Also known as **serialism**. **23, 24**

20th century art music Classical music composed in the 20th century. Used ideas such as **atonality**, **whole tone scales**, **serialism** and **microtonality**. **22-24**

A

air guitar A term used to describe the playing of an imaginary guitar. **47**

alap The first phase of a typical **raga** performance. Improvised, doesn't have a beat. Played on the sitar, with just the tambura for accompaniment. **29**

arpeggio The notes of a chord played in succession, either going up or down. **35**

appoggiatura One of the notes in a chord can be split into two notes — the note itself and the one just above or below it (the **appoggiatura**). The appoggiatura's played first and clashes with the rest of the chord, then the note in the chord is played (the resolution). **21, 34**

appraising your performance 3

appraising your composition 6

atonality Using notes that aren't from any particular key. Commonly used in **20th century art music**. 22

B

ballad A type of folk song that tells a story. **16**

bandish A song that forms the final phase of a **raga** performance. Also known as **gat** if it's played only on instruments (without voice). **29**

baroque Musical style of the seventeenth and early eighteenth centuries. Strong bass and lots of ornamentation.

    baroque melody 17
    baroque structure 18-19
    baroque melody patterns 20-21

bass guitar Guitar with 4 strings tuned to E, A, D and G, with the bottom E being 1½ octaves below middle C. Used to pick out individual notes of a bass line. **37**

Bhangra Modern bhangra is a fusion of traditional Indian and Pakistani music with club-style dance music. **43**

binary forms Form of music in 2 distinct sections. **18, 35**

blues Style of 20th century music developed in America with a distinctive scale and swinging rhythm. **25-26**
See also **12-bar blues**. **26**

brass Family of wind instruments including trumpet, trombone, tuba and French horn. **10, 11, 13, 37**

British folk music Traditional British music played by ordinary people, including things like worksongs, ballads and Morris dancing music. **16, 39**

C

call A short melody, followed by a **response**, that together gives the feeling of a 'question and answer'. Can be on instruments or voice. Often features in **12-bar blues**. **26, 40**

ceremonial dance Traditional dance for important occasions. **31**

chaconne A type of **baroque** dance in **ground bass** form. **19**

chitarrone See **theorbo**. **33**

Chopin 19th century Polish composer, famous for piano pieces. **39**

chord patterns 8

chromatics Notes that don't belong to the main key of a melody. **21-23, 34**

classical Either any music that's not pop (or jazz, folk, hip-hop, R&B, etc.) or music composed in Europe in the late 18th and early 19th centuries.

    classical melody 17
    classical structure 18-19
    classical melody patterns 20-21

clave rhythm The basic rhythm of a piece of son or salsa music around which the rest of the music has to fit. **40**

cluster chords Chords with notes really close together. **24**

coda Bit at the end of a song that's different from the rest, and finishes it off nicely. **35**

composing to your instrument 11

composition 4-6, 11

composition (the brief) 4

consort A band of musicians which accompanied posh court dances such as the **pavan** and **galliard**. **33**

contour How the pitch changes — e.g. big leaps between notes, going through the notes of a chord etc. **14**

Glossary and Index

counter melody Extra tune played at the same time as the theme to make sure things don't get boring. **19**

coursework 1

court dance Dance for celebrating official occasions like coronations or royal weddings. **31, 32**

crumhorn Wooden wind instrument, curved at one end like a walking stick, with a double reed like an oboe. Also sometimes spelt krummhorn. **33**

D

dance music 16, 31-38

Debussy French composer who wrote melodies with a **whole tone scale**. **22, 39**

disco music He's a complicated man, and no one understands him but his woman... Shaft **36-37**

Dorian mode A set of eight notes, represented by playing the notes D to D on the white keys of a keyboard. **15**

drone notes Umm... Notes that drone on under the main melody. Often found in **Indian classical music** such as **raga**. **27, 29**

drum machines Electronic instruments used instead of live drums. Often used on glitterball-tastic disco tunes. **37**

duple metre Metre used in dance, with 2 beats per bar. **31**

E

electric guitar Like a normal guitar, but only noisy when you plug it into an amplifier. Then they can be *really* noisy. Trust me. **37**

evaluating your performance 3

F

families of instruments Groups of similar instruments, e.g. woodwind, brass, strings, percussion, ~~Addams~~. **10**

folk dance Traditional dances performed at public events, such as Morris dancing and maypole dancing. **31**

front line The players who stand at the front in a jazz or salsa band and play the tune. Usually sax/trumpet/clarinet. **41**

further coursework 1

fusion Creating a new style of music by combining two or more existing styles. **39**

G

galliard A dance in **triple metre** with a controlled **tempo**, played by a **consort**. See also **pavan**. **32-33**

gat A song that forms the final phase of a **raga** performance, played on instruments rather than sung. Known as a **bandish** if it's sung. **29**

gharana School of players teaching **raga**, a form of **Indian classical music**. **27**

ground bass A way of playing variations with a strong repeating bass part as the main **theme**. **19**

H

harmony Everyone getting on. Peace and love. The end of war and strife. Erm... I mean to say: Two parts of music harmonise when they go together nicely. Sometimes the backing, or accompanying part, is called the harmony. **17**

harpsichord A keyboard instrument shaped like a grand piano. It was popular in **Baroque** times. **17**

I

imitation A phrase is repeated with little variations. Could be one instrument or voice, or two or more, imitating each other. **20**

Indian classical music Classical music from... surprise, surprise... India. **Raga** is the only type of Indian classical music you need to learn about. **27**

instrumental dance music Music written in the style of a dance, but made for listening, not for actual dancing. **31**

integrated coursework 1

intro (introduction) Opening bit of a song or piece (especially in sonata form). **36**

J

jazz Music with lots of syncopation, improvisation and quirky harmonisation. You know it when you hear it. **40**

jhala The third phase of a typical **raga** performance. Faster than the **alap** and **jhor**. **29**

jhor The second phase of a typical **raga** performance. Improvised, played on the sitar, with just the tambura for accompaniment. Faster and more rhythmic than the **alap**. **29**

K

komal A note played slightly flat in some **ragas**. **28**

Glossary and Index

Glossary and Index

rhythm section Instruments which keep the rhythm in, for example, a jazz or salsa band. An example of a rhythm section might be a double bass, drum kit and guitar. **41**

riff Repeated phrase played over and over again. Mostly used in pop, rock and jazz. **41**

Romantic composers Composers from 1820 to 1900 such as Schumann, Chopin, Verdi and Puccini. They used a lot of **chromatic** notes. **22, 35**

rondo forms A way of structuring music so you start with one tune, go on to a new one, go back to the first one, on to another new one, back to the first one, on to a new one... as many times as you like. **18**

rumba Cuban dance with a similar rhythm to **son**. **40**

S

salsa A type of Latin American dance music. It is a fusion of **jazz** and Cuban **son** style music. Salsa tunes have three main parts: a verse, a montuno (chorus) and the mambo (a break from the main tune). **39-42**

scale A set pattern of notes all from the same key. The most common ones in western music are major and minor scales. **9, 22, 25**

Schoenberg Austrian composer who came up with a way of structuring atonal music, called the 12-note system, or **serialism**. **23-24**

section A group of musical phrases. The way sections are put together gives music its overall **structure**. **14**

semitone The smallest interval between notes on a piano. Modern major **scales** have a semitone gap between notes 7 and 8. **15, 24**

sequencing Repeating phrases but changing the pitch. The intervals between notes stay the same. **20**

sequencer Computerised equipment for recording snippets of music, played in loops as a backing track. Often used in funky disco music. **37**

serialism The 12-note system created by **Schoenberg** in the 1920s, which involves rearranging the 12 chromatic notes of an octave into a set order. **23, 24**

short song Type of folk music with romantic or comic lyrics. **16**

sitar Large, long-necked string instrument used in **Indian Classical Music** such as **raga**, with between 4 and 7 strings. Up to 5 strings are plucked for the **melody** and the other 2 create **drone notes**. **27, 28**

social dance Dance which takes place in a ballroom/ parish hall/disco/club. **31**

son Cuban dance music style which had a big influence on **salsa** music. **40, 41**

sonata form Piece of music with two main themes. These are introduced in the first bit, developed in the middle bit and repeated in the last bit. **17**

stimuli (rhythmic ideas) Starting points such as a pattern of notes or a chord pattern given to you in the **terminal task**. **8**

Strauss (Johann, Johann the Younger, Josef, Eduard) Viennese family who all composed **waltzes**. Johann the Younger composed 'The Blue Danube', among others. **34-35**

strings Group of instruments with... like... strings. The jury's still out on whether pianos count. **10, 11, 13**

structure The way a piece of music is organised. **9, 18-19**

syncopation Rhythmic technique where the accents are shifted from the main beat to a weaker beat, to avoid a regular rhythm. E.g. in $\frac{4}{4}$ time the main accent would usually fall on the first beat — whereas in syncopated $\frac{4}{4}$ time you could move the accent to, say, the second beat. **25, 41**

T

tabla Pair of drums used in **Indian classical music** such as **raga**. **27, 28**

tabor Small drum hung round the neck and played with one hand. Played as a pair with a **pipe**. **33**

tala Rhythm in **Indian classical music** with a set number of beats, played on the **tabla**. **28**

tambura Similar in shape to a **sitar**, but with only four metal strings. Used as a backing instrument in **Indian classical music**. **27, 29**

tango Dance with a set rhythm and movements. Or a sickly fizzy drink. **31**

tempo Speed. **19, 31**

terminal task **8-9**

ternary form Piece in three sections. The first and last are much the same. The middle one's a bit different and in a different (but related) key. **18, 35**

theme Musical idea. The one you hum. **19**

theorbo A really big **lute** used to play the bass line for **pavan** and **galliard** dances. Sometimes called the **chitarrone**. **33**

timbre The kind of sound an instrument makes — e.g. woody, soft, mellow, reedy. **10, 22**

tivra A note played slightly sharp in some **ragas**. **28**

tonal Music where the key it's written in gives it a definite character. **22**

transposing instruments Instruments tuned to keys other than concert pitch. Transposing instruments are mainly **brass** or **woodwind**. **11, 12**

tremolo Play in a trembly, nervous-sounding way. **35**

Glossary and Index

Cut Out and Keep Bagpipers

As a parting gift, I'd like to leave you with this picture of two fine bagpipers. Of course, if you *do* decide to cut it out, you'll lose half the S and T sections of the glossary. Hmm... didn't quite think that one through.